SOMETHING'S LOST AND MUST BE FOUND

Seven Short Tales of Inspiration on a Long Leash

Lisa Begin-Kruysman

For Cathy,

From one dog lover
to another.

Yours in Dog,
Lisa Begin-Kruysman

Cover Photo Credit - Roger Heykoop

ISBN: 978-1-463-74045-0

For Richard, Keeper of the Faith

Preface

Something's Lost and Must be Found
~Seven Short Tails of Inspiration on a Long Leash~

The seven short tales in this collection were written by a dog-lover to be enjoyed by those who cherish or are guardians of man's best friends. Each story stands alone, connected only by a theme of things "lost and found." In each instance characters find resolution through the help of some search and rescue dogs of the soul; a mother coping with a tragic loss, a father trying to reconnect with his son, a teen-age girl dealing with some weighty issues, a jobless young man attempting to regain his humanity, a single woman searching for self-worth, and a loyal dog-owner watching over his beloved dog that is searching for his "true and happy home."

These stories evoke that feeling a human gets when after letting a dog off-leash to run freely, their best furry friend returns for a mini-reunion, requesting to be led back home. At that moment all is right in the world. Even those who aren't among the legion of dog-loving Americans can make a personal connection with these stories, one that resonates in some area of their life.

In this edition, I am happy to present a seventh "tail," Still Life with Dog in Red Collar, an updated version of a story that was awarded an Honorable Mention in the 75th Annual Writer's Digest Competition.

About the Author

Lisa Begin-Kruysman lives in Ocean County, New Jersey, with her husband Rich and Portuguese water dog, Hooper. Her short fiction has garnered national recognition in writing competitions sponsored by Calliope Writers and Writer's Digest Magazine.

In 2010, the author launched a blog dedicated to the venerable National Dog Week Movement established in 1928. With over one-hundred posts to-date, she has learned that now, more than ever, there is a need for an intelligent exchange about the state of the dog in the states of the nation.

To learn more about National Dog Week, please go to: http://nationaldogweekbook.wordpress.com. In an informed and enlightened world, every dog can have its day and hopefully its week, too.

Acknowledgements

I would like to thank my husband Rich for all his help and support over the past several years, even during the "ruffest" of times. Thanks also to friend and fellow-author, David Lender, for inspiring me to join the ranks of the electronically published.

A thank you also goes to my sister, Manette Begin-Loudon, for her encouragement and to my parents, Jack and Cindy, for their constant support over the years.

And a special acknowledgement is extended to Marilyn Green whose chance encounter with me influenced the development of this book, and to Saint Anthony of Padua, the patron soul of lost items, the poor and travelers and a devoted disciple of Saint Francis of Assisi, patron saint of animals.

Try to be the god on earth, the all-powerful and all-mighty your dog thinks you are. Never let him learn his mistake.

Will Judy, Founder of the *National Dog Week Movement*

Something's Lost and Must be Found

Antonio, a seven-year old Havanese dog, was an Easter gift from my husband. Like a holiday bunny, he arrived in my life presented in an oversized basket surrounded by dog treats and plush toys, a rescue from the local shelter.

The Havanese, bred for companionship, was a clever choice on my husband's part. It is said to be the sturdiest of the Toy Group, a small dog with a big attitude and huge heart with a great capacity for love. But all that would be wasted on me.

"Look how cute he is," my husband had proclaimed, lifting the dog up close to my face for my inspection and acceptance.

The shaggy little dog pressed its moist black nose to mine offering my cheek a quick lick with his pink tongue the color of bubble gum; his alert amber eyes burned into mine. When Antonio was placed in my arms he burrowed in my chest. I quickly returned him to my husband before his heartbeat could match the rhythm of mine.

My heart. That was the problem. The dog seemed to sense its heaviness, its loneliness. It was a place that had been closed to outsiders for over three years. This little dog would open shut doors boarded up with two-by-fours, sealed off with crime-scene tape, embedded with booby traps for good measure; devices meant to keep excavators and explorers out.

Sensing my reluctance to bond with the dog, my husband took a non-committal approach. "Let's keep him for a while and see how it goes. He needs us."

But I had no intention of keeping this fifteen pound black and white ball of fur that had been tossed like a life-line to a swimmer drowning in angry waters, going down for the last time. This victim did not want to be rescued, preferring instead to be swallowed up by the sea, assaulted by rogue waves and a current of salty tears. And she certainly did not want to rescue or be rescued by a dog. Yes, this dog was a clever way of coaxing me back to the land of the living, an offering to someone who had suffered the worst possible tragedy, the loss of a child.

"Maybe he's a lost dog, somebody might be looking for him right now," I said.

"He's been at the shelter for over a month, surrendered by his owner. It's their loss as far as I'm concerned."

Antonio, or Tony as he would come to be called, was just the first strategy in the reversal of what was perceived as my process of shutting down. The second part involved a long drive to a coastal resort town in northern Florida several hours away. A trip to get me away from a place that housed a monument of misery; the backyard swimming pool where I had discovered the body of my two-year old son floating face down over three summers before.

"What joy or comfort can a trip near the water or a homeless dog bring me?" I'd demanded of my husband.

"You need to…" he'd paused. "You need to move on, to live for something again."

I hated his words. My self-inflicted punishment was to remain in this house forever, with a daily reminder of my uselessness as a human being. And the thought of being responsible for something again, even a pet, scared me to the core. But instead of saying that, I shot him a snarky question, "What if I don't want to move on?"

He'd sighed saying, "You're stuck. No one, including me, seems to know what you need anymore. All I know is you've lost something, we've lost something and I don't know if we can get it back."

"Yes, that something we lost was our son, our only child," I snapped.

But I knew he was talking about something else, something less defined; my isolation, my separation from the living, my loss of purpose.

In the days following Antonio's entrance into our lives, my days were carefully shaped by his care. I went through the motion of being a good dog owner; I walked, fed and brushed him, but did not allow him to bond with me. Then my hours became absorbed with packing for the trip, a suitcase for me and a doggy travel bag with a little brush, treats and leash for Antonio.

The ride south from New Jersey through the Carolinas along I-95 is an ever-changing landscape. Until well past Washington DC, my view was occupied by urban sprawl filled with homes, offices and strip malls built on every available inch of land and highways packed with commuter traffic. Passing south of Fredericksburg, Virginia, brought rural stretches where small ranch-style brick homes with carports sat next to service roads and Visitor Welcome Centers offered free maps and motel discount coupons with designated dog walking areas. During our stops, Antonio would sniff the ground, deciphering the secret code of the traveling canines who had come before.

Throughout North Carolina, towering billboards bombarded us with advertising for a tourist attraction with a south of the border theme; a hokey road-side stop featuring an arcade, hotel, restaurant and rides complete with a tower topped by a giant sombrero.

"Pedro Corny?" My husband read the words of each sign to me, followed a few miles later by another. "Fill your trunk with Pedro's Junk." "Who writes this stuff?" he wondered out loud, trying to lighten the mood in the car. "Come and wet your whee-zle at our Cantina," he read one more with a groan.

We arrived at our rented condo by late afternoon. "There's still time to take Antonio for a quick walk on the beach," my husband said with forced cheer, trying hard to fill the air with positive energy.

Afterward, while I cooked the pink shrimp we'd bought at a little stand on the way into town, he unloaded the car. Tony dutifully followed him with each trip to and from the car, watching attentively as his new master unpacked suitcases, storing them in a large closet in an unused guest room of the condo.

"Dinner's ready," I called shortly after, setting out large plates of shrimp and rice and glasses of chilled white wine. We settled down to eat, but something wasn't right.

"Where's Tony?" I asked. We called for the little dog, typically underfoot when food was in the picture.

"Tony?" we called again. "Where are you?" our yells echoed throughout the condo. "Did you leave him outside?" I asked. We rushed out, tracing the route to the car. While my husband checked out the lot and the inside of the car for good measure, I scanned the horizon near the shoreline then eyed the shadows and hidden places flanking a row of condos. In the gloom of the early evening each unit looked exactly alike. With each passing minute my stomach tightened in an all too familiar way. I felt as though the ground below me would start to quake, toppling the protective walls I had so carefully built around me. I knew I should never have accepted this dog, or come to this place.

Back inside the condo we made a quick check of the rooms. No sign, no sound. On the counter, the uneaten food had grown cold in the darkened kitchen. Paranoia and fear set in. "Someone took him," I blurted out, panicking. "Those kids in the next condo were paying way too much attention to him." I referred to a group of young college-age spring breakers occupying the rental unit next to ours.

Resuming our outside search, I was discreetly spying into neighboring windows when a condominium security van rolled by. We waved it down. The gum-chewing "guard" listened without expression as we stated our predicament. "Saw a dog like that up the road a piece this afternoon," he said.

"Why didn't you stop and get him?" I asked.

He shrugged answering, "Some dogs around here run around free all the time."

With that news our inside search was suspended. "He has a collar with a name tag, if he's found someone will call so make sure you keep your cell close by," my husband tried to assure me. "I'm going to take a ride around."

Restless, I paced the condo grounds calling Tony's name until I was hoarse. In time, other vacationers and locals joined in.

"Bobcats got him, I bet," I heard one woman comment to another. "They can take a little dog like that right down when they hunt in pairs."

Her friend replied, "I saw a Boston terrier lying on the side of the road yesterday. Run right over."

In the dark, cries of "Tony" rang out until well after nine o'clock. With no sight of the little dog and with none during my husband's countless drive-by searches, we hoped for more luck the next day and settled in for a restless night.

I didn't sleep much. Images of Tony's little body in the jaws of a wildcat or floating in the ocean flooded my mind. I found myself reaching for the phone to call a friend for emotional support, but couldn't. Like I had in the recent past, I remained covered up by a blanket of isolation surfing through late night talk shows, twenty-four hour shopping networks and old movie channels, watching none. "Tony, where are you?" I asked out loud in the dark. No answer. I had failed again, as a protector, as a caregiver, as a mother.

The next day brought calls to two animal shelters, three neighboring condo associations and three major resorts in the area in the event Tony had gone looking for food or shelter. 'Lost Dog' flyers were posted throughout the immediate area.

"Why couldn't you have been more careful?" I asked my husband. "How could you have left him alone outside?"

"I thought he was in the house with you," he shot back.

This accusatory exchange had a ring of unwelcome familiarity. Agitated and wracked with worry, I couldn't sit still. I exited the condo, slamming the door behind me. Overhead, a turkey vulture circled; I tried not to imagine the worst.

I walked down the road calling "Tony, Tony," like a robotic recording, wandering down to the shoreline where happy beachgoers and their dogs scurried and skidded in the sand, darting in and out of the foamy residue of receding waves. Scanning the horizon I hoped for a glimpse of

Antonio, trying not to think of his fate if he'd been pulled out to sea by the tide.

Not ready to return home, I left the beach, traveling on a path that led away from the condo. Above me, twisted branches of Live Oak dripping with feathery grey Spanish moss arched and met forming a canopy. In the dark tunnel of trees I cursed this place, a place I had trusted to help me heal, no longer a last resort for hope; but a tourist trap of lost souls.

What had happened to my heart? I wondered bitterly. It had become so hardened that I'd been unable to offer love to a poor little dog when he'd needed it most. Now I would probably never get another chance.

At the end of the wooded path, I'd drifted into a sun-filled cul-de-sac just a half-mile or so from the rental property. Filled with homes perched on manicured lawns, smiling people walked their happy dogs and all was right in a world where nothing ever got lost or died; a place that seemed to mock me.

In the window of one home, a large shepherd-mix barked at me. Without warning, my legs gave way. Exhausted, I slumped down into the cool green lawn, landing cross-legged on a stranger's front yard.

From inside, the barking grew louder, like an alarm. The front door opened and the big dog ran for me and began licking at my face. "Can I help you?" a woman's voice asked. Its calm concerned tone brought a river of tears that ran down my face and watered her lawn.

She led me inside. Regaining some composure, I told her about Antonio's disappearance, and our futile search. Reaching for her car keys and some tissues, she said, "Let's take a ride with Sonny, he knows where all the dogs like to hang out don't you boy?" As we drove up and down winding back roads the attentive dog poked his head out the window as if assisting in our mission, his shepherd instincts showing.

At first this woman and I made small talk; how she had adopted Sonny from a local shelter, how dog-friendly the area was, how dogs went missing all the time, but were found safely. Her reassuring manner and the gentle hum of the car's engine eased the tension in my neck and back.

I was so relaxed in fact that when she asked about my family I found myself blurting out the details of the tragic incident that had changed my life. From finding my boy's lifeless body afloat in our pool, the police, the medical examiners, the ambulance and the hysterical crowd that had gathered, no detail was spared. I spoke about the endless stream of hopeless dark days that followed each one more difficult than the next. She listened without comment as we drove, finally pulling the car back into her driveway after an hour of fruitless searching.

"I don't know if you're a betting woman, but I'm willing to wager that your dog is somewhere close to where you're staying, hiding, just waiting for you to find him. He may think he's back in the shelter and he's shut down and depressed."

Her words made me feel worse. With the way I had behaved, why shouldn't he be depressed? I thanked her for her help and time and for listening; I reluctantly exited the car and turned to leave.

"I don't know if you're a praying woman, but here's something you might try," she continued.

I looked at her expectantly.

"You can recite a prayer to St. Anthony, the patron saint of lost things. There are different versions of it, but I like the one that goes, Tony, Tony come around, something's lost and must be found." She smiled and added, "Sometimes you find things you didn't even know were missing."

I got the feeling she wasn't talking about glasses or keys. I promised to let her know if Tony, the dog or saint, showed up.

Returning to an empty condo, I found my husband was out on patrol again. The sky had clouded over; a storm was moving in as another day came to a close. I tried to choke down a bit of food, but couldn't.

In the dining room I poured myself a big glass of wine and stared out a window; palm fronds fluttered in the strengthening breeze. The empty condo pool with its clear blue water contrasted with our pool at home now covered tightly with a tarp that was pocked with puddles of brown water and dead leaves.

The comparison struck me; the water in the pool before me now rippling with heavy raindrops was the water of renewal, revival, a source of recreation, not a taker of life as I had come to regard it.

I recalled the "Tony" prayer and only then did my weary brain get the connection. "Tony Tony, come around, something's lost and must be found." I whispered. Although it was a prayer intended for a patron saint, I spoke it as if I was talking to the dog, my dog. I realized then that in his finding I might have a chance at living again.

"Tony, Tony," I began again, louder this time. I finished the verse repeating it several times. Outside, the weather grew turbulent; blinds rattled over open windows. I pictured my husband driving around shouting Tony's name through an open car window, his voice muffled by the gusting wind.

From the back of the condo a door slammed. Clear as day, the image of a closet in a darkened room appeared in my mind. Without delay I ran down the hall. Opening the door to an unused room, I noticed for the first time the outline of a closet obscured in darkness. Pulling the closet door open, Tony impatiently brushed past my legs. He proceeded to relieve himself on the ceramic tile floor not once, but twice.

He looked up at me, head cocked questioningly as if to say, "Where have you been?" Then he ran down the hall to a water bowl and drank for what seemed like forever. When I sat next to him on the kitchen floor he jumped into my arms, licking at the tears on my face.

He had been trapped in that closet, stored away alongside the empty luggage. "Why didn't you cry, or whine, or try to scratch your way out?" I implored.

He clung to me; his heart beat matching mine which was no longer closed to him. Gone were the barriers, and protective walls.

From down the hall I heard the front door open. "In here," I called from the kitchen.

"Looks like you found something," my husband said joining us on the floor, his eyes filled with relief and a hundred questions.

There would be time to talk about the details later; time to go and thank my guardian angel down the road and her dog and of course to give thanks to St. Anthony, patron St. of "The Lost."

For now, it was enough to be in the moment, caught up in the current of a life moving forward. In my heart, Antonio had found a new home, and in his presence, I would live again.

"Yes," I answered. "And our dog's come back, too."

Grooming Conversation

Drip. Drop. A bathtub full of tepid water accepts a few strays from a leaky faucet. Sammy, a big Golden Retriever gently pants nearby, patiently awaiting a much-needed bath. Along with the plumbing, the poor dog's grooming has been neglected. I make a mental note to fix that leak as I kneel next to Sammy, removing his worn leather collar and his red bandana thickly coated with long reddish strands.

"Good boy," I whisper rubbing the unfettered neck of the eight-year old family pet.

Family pet? I think to myself. There was a time, not too long ago, when this duty of dog grooming was relegated to my son, Jake. After all, Sammy is technically his dog, a gift for Jake's sixth birthday. Now at age fourteen, Jake doesn't have too much time for Sammy, or me, for that matter.

This thought gets me worked up. "Jake!" I call out the bathroom door. I wait a few moments and then call again. Lately I think I'd have a better chance of communicating with my son through a text message or an e-mail. "Jake," I try again.

Jake's lanky outline finally appears at the bathroom door, ear buds and a cell phone attached to his head and hand like appendages. "Yeah, Dad, what's up?"

"Would you mind helping me wash your dog?" I shout, motioning for him to remove the plugs from his ears.

Jake reluctantly relinquishes his IPOD and cell phone, placing both on a laundry hamper in the corner of the room. Stripped of his electronic armor he looks vulnerable and awkward, alone in this quiet room with his father. Jake drops to his knees and joins me. He picks up Sammy's brush and without much enthusiasm runs it over the dog's back.

Instead of reprimanding Jake for his lack of responsibility I remain quiet, fostering a glimmer of hope that I might have the opportunity for an actual conversation with my son. For good measure I visualize an imaginary harness placed around his chest, attached to a retractable leash.

Sammy, responding to this unexpected attention from my son, dispenses two well-placed licks on Jake's chin. For the first time Jake smiles.

"Look. He misses you."

"I'm around," Jake snaps, his smile vanishing.

Easy, I coach myself. I let out some of the imaginary leash.

From on top of the hamper Jake's cell phone buzzes like a cicada on a hot June sidewalk. He stops brushing, staring at his phone as a text message is delivered. It takes all his strength not to pounce on it like a cat on a field mouse.

I tighten up on the leash, distracting him with a question. "How's that algebra coming along?"

Jake is examining Sammy's left ear. "Okay, I guess," the standard answer is dispatched, followed by a few seconds of dead silence as he examines the dog's big head.

Then something happens; Jake initiates a dialogue. "Remember the time that stupid Boxer bit Sammy right here? Look, you can still see the scar," he says stroking the dog's notched ear.

"Yeah, I sure do. That dog ambushed poor Sammy," I answer, carefully letting up on the leash a bit, allowing Jake to take the lead of our conversation.

Jake reacts with a sudden outburst. "Yeah, that dog was a bully. Just like those kids at school who won't leave my friend, Tommy alone. Why do they have to call him stupid names, and take things out of his locker all the time?"

In his agitated state, Jake yanks hard with the brush at the fur on Sammy's rump. Sammy lets out a small whimper. "Easy," I say, calming Jake and comforting Sammy without interrupting the moment.

Jake abruptly changes the subject while apologetically smoothing the dog's roughened haunches with his hands. "Yesterday my algebra teacher, Mrs. Lerner, said I need a tutor if I want to be an architect some day," he continues to talk freely. "I got a C plus on my test the other day. But apparently that's not good enough for her."

"Well it is better than a D," I say, making a small attempt at humor, pulling back on the virtual leash, drawing him a little closer to me. An increasingly impatient Sammy stands up and arches his back with a prolonged yawn. With my index finger I test the bath water's temperature trying to buy some time.

"My friend John's uncle has to go back to Iraq next month," Jake continues to air his grievances now sputtering like a long dormant volcano. "He's in the army and he just got back from being there for two years. It's not fair, he has two little kids and they need him at home."

"I'm sorry to hear that. I hope that terrible war ends soon," is all I can think to say.

Sammy slumps to the floor with a sigh. Then he rolls over, soliciting a belly rub from Jake who quickly obliges.

"You want to be an architect?" I ask, bringing the subject back to my son. I recall that just last month it was a Crime Scene Investigator.

"Yeah, maybe we should get me a tutor," Jake says, speaking to me over the dog's underside.

As if on cue, Sammy sits up as though he knows the water is ready for him. No more stalling. I know this moment will come to an end very shortly. I let out the leash to its full capacity as Jake's cell phone hums again.

"My girlfriend Julie's mother had to have some kind of cancer test. Her operation was this morning," he explains with his eyes glued to the phone. "I hope she's going to be okay."

Off comes the invisible collar, and leash. I release my son from his duties, breaking off our connection. "Take your message. I'll give Sammy his bath."

"Thanks Dad," Jake says. Smiling, he places a big kiss on the top of Sammy's head. Then he spontaneously hugs me around the neck before snatching up his phone and IPOD, disappearing down the hall.

"Let's not let Sammy's grooming go for so long next time, okay?" I call after him, but he is gone, reclaimed by the surprisingly complicated matters of his teen-age life.

As the last of the bath water swooshes loudly down the drain I help the clumsy dog from the tub, savoring the words that still hang in the air. In the unlikely space of a bathroom I had briefly captured one of those rare head-to-head moments with my son; sitting around a crackling campfire, baiting a fish hook, soothing a bruised knee suffered during his first solo bike ride, and now grooming the family dog; each presenting an opportunity to communicate, to practice the lost art of conversation.

War, bullies, cancer, career and a girlfriend. Who knows what concerns go through a kid's head if we don't ever get the opportunity to talk to them?

With a large towel I dry the big dog giving him a full body hug. Then I speak to the clueless canine, "Thanks, Sammy. You were great!" Sammy regales me with an impromptu shower as he wildly shakes off the excess bath water.

Later that afternoon, I replace Sammy's collar and attach his leash. It's a warm spring day and the newly clean and dry Sammy needs a walk. Nearing a park, Sammy strains on his chain eager to join a group of young children and their parents on the playground. The youngsters chatter away noisily, eager for the attention of their caretakers who are too absorbed with talking to each other, or reading the day's news. "Listen to your kids now," I want to tell them, "They won't always want to talk to you."

Sammy yanks again, harder. If I let him off-leash I know he will skip the playground and head straight to the red soil of a nearby baseball diamond, indulging in a luxurious dirt bath.

"No, boy," I command, holding tight to his leash. "Not today, you just got all nice and clean. Maybe in a few days."

Sammy whines in protest and a pleasant prospect pops into my head. Then I smile, anticipating just how filthy Sammy can get in that dirt and the inevitable grooming session it will bring about; another chance for a real conversation with my son over the haunches and under the belly of a wordless, but wonderful family friend

Losing the Wait

The headline of the Lifestyle section of the morning newspaper caught my eye. 'New Study finds Fifteen Percent of American Teens are Overweight.'

Plop. As if on cue a blob of raspberry filling oozed from the half-eaten jelly doughnut dangling from my hand. It landed right on top of the word 'Fifteen." But no amount of sugary goo could coat the sad fact; I was fifteen and part of that hefty fifteen percent.

Splat. Another bright red glop landed on the kitchen floor right next to my foot. Not missing a beat, my dog Flora rushed over cleaning up the mess faster than a wet vac. For good measure she licked my big toe. Satisfied she hadn't missed anything the drooling dog waddled away and flopped back down on the floor.

From upstairs my mother called. "Sara. Don't forget to feed Flora."

Don't worry, I thought. Neither one of us looked like we ever forgot to eat.

I threw the newspaper with its stupid statistics in the trash; the uneaten part of my jelly donut quickly followed, powder and all. But those extra calories and that depressing fact would stay with me all day. I knew I needed to lose weight and I really wanted to. I was just waiting for the right time; my next birthday, New Year's Day, summertime or maybe my next move to a new town or city.

My father's job transfers had caused my family to move three times in the past ten years. Until now they had been to climates where the weather remained cool enough most of the time to keep me covered up; places like New England and the mid-west.

But my luck had run out. This time I had landed in sunny southern California, land of the slim and toned and barely clothed. Thankfully it was June at the time of my arrival and school was out for the summer. Once again, I set a goal for myself; I had over two months to lose the weight before the awkward start of yet another new school.

My parents tried to help. "Maybe you could join a gym, take up swimming, or tennis," my mother suggested.

"How about walking? When I was your age we walked everywhere," my father said.

But the thought of a chunky teenager lumbering alone through the manicured suburbs of Orange County was out of the question. No one seemed to walk anywhere around here and I was already different enough, thank you.

And there would be no health club for me. The only club I cared to belong to was the Refrigerator Club. With the opening of its door I could find my true friends among the shelves. Here all members of the major food groups accepted me. I was cool in more ways than one.

Besides food, my only other close companion was Flora, my sweet pug. She had been a gift for my tenth birthday, a gift to help soften the news of yet another move to yet another new state.

But lately I noticed that even Flora, now five years old, was getting bigger. At Flora's annual check-up the next day, the veterinarian confirmed this. "Whoa!" she said, struggling to lift Flora onto the examination table. "What are you feeding this dog?"

Embarrassed, I felt my face turning bright red. Apparently even dogs had to be skinny here.

"A dog that's fit and trim can add up to a year and a half to its life," she continued. She recommended a special dog food and gave me a measuring cup. "And let's get some exercise." She kept her eyes on Flora, but I knew she was also talking to me. "Be firm with her. No table food and easy on the treats."

That day I knew I couldn't wait any longer. If I didn't want to lose the weight for myself, I'd do it for my best friend; she had no choice and her life depended on it.

Flora and I walked for ten minutes on our first day. It was a start. Each time out, we would add another block. By the second week we were up to thirty minutes a day.

I began to see the same people on our daily route. Some even seemed to look for us. One of them was Mrs. Adelman, an elderly woman who lived one block over. She sat alone at her front window each day. Her yipping Yorkshire terrier seemed to be her only companion.

"Excuse me," she called over to me one afternoon. "Would you be able to walk my dog, Bunny?" she asked. "She really needs to get out. You seem to be so good with your dog. I'll pay you of course." Mrs. Adelman explained she was recovering from hip surgery. "Poor Bunny. I used to walk her so much," she said.

It must have been in some other place. Around here dogs, much like their humans, didn't seem to walk anywhere. Enclosed in large backyards, they barked constantly and dug useless holes under tall fences to occupy their long lonely boring days.

That night at dinner I told my parents about Mrs. Adelman's request. They thought it would be a good idea. But we agreed I wouldn't take any money from her.

Within a few days Bunny and Flora became fast friends. And they would make several new ones.

The woman, who lived in the big stucco house next to Mrs. Adelman, soon sought my services. "Hey," she called me over to her door one morning. "I always see you walking your dogs. I was wondering if I could hire you to walk mine. I've been so busy lately. Tiny is a good boy, but he could use some socialization."

A huge dog quietly pushed its way past his owner and joined us outside on the stoop. He stood silently by my side, the top of his head nestled under my armpit.

"Tiny is a Tibetan Mastiff," she said. "Don't worry, he just looks scary. He's really a gentle giant. They're really very spiritual dogs." As if on cue, Tiny licked me right across my face with his giant tongue. "You can handle him."

It was official; I had my first paying customer. My new dog-walking job had some extra benefits, too. I started to stay away from my meetings with the Refrigerator Club and I could now pass a fast food restaurant without going inside. Thanks to Bunny, Tiny and Flora I couldn't even if I'd wanted to. I noticed I was tightening my belt a little more each week.

But Tiny's size and strength was too much for me. I had to start walking him alone. With that big dog by my side my confidence grew. I began walking further from home, bravely exploring new neighborhoods.

One late afternoon Tiny and I wandered into a section of town filled with older homes, most looked like they needed a lot of fixing-up. Here chain link fences choked with weeds were posted with signs that warned No Trespassing and Beware of Dog. "Maybe we should put that sign around your neck," I joked to Tiny.

On a certain block of this broken-down place, one shabby house stood out; so run-down, I thought it was abandoned. I was about to turn and leave when I noticed a dog chained to a fence that surrounded the yard. The dog's black and tan fur was flattened in sweat against his skinny body. His rib cage was disturbingly visible.

Tiny and I approached slowly.

"Hi there, fella," I whispered when he stuck his warm nose through a link in the fence. His sad dark eyes met mine. They told of hands that slapped instead of stroked, and voices that scolded, but never soothed. Tiny watched him carefully as the thirsty dog gulped from the water bottle I offered him. The sun was setting now and I knew I needed to leave. "Bye for now. We'll bring you a treat tomorrow," I promised.

But on our next visit the dog was not alone.

"Hello," a little girl greeted us as we approached. She sat alone of the front steps of the house, barefoot and dressed in a faded yellow sundress. Her uncombed blond hair hung over her face. She looked to be no more than five years old.

"Hi there," I answered. I looked for an adult, but no one else appeared. "My name is Sara. And this is Tiny." I remained outside the fence, speaking to her from the sidewalk. The brown and tan dog slept under her feet.

"Tiny?" she giggled. "He's as big as a pony."

"Where's your mommy?" I asked.

She answered quickly. "She's sleeping,"

"What's your dog's name?" I asked as I fished inside the pockets of my jeans for a dog treat.

"Which one? We have lots of dogs."

But our talk came to a rude end as the front screen door burst open. An angry woman rushed down the steps running right toward me. "What do you want?" she said.

From behind heavily curtained windows a muffled mix of yipping and howling escaped. Tiny responded with a low, warning growl. The menacing woman returned to the stoop, yanking the little girl by the arm. She pointed at me and shouted. "Get out of here, and don't come back. You people should just leave us alone."

Her once quiet dog was now up on its hind legs barking fiercely, still secured by a long chain to the fence. But his fury was directed at the woman. I dropped a biscuit under the fence and backed off, wondering what she had meant by "you people."

Back in my own neighborhood I returned Tiny to his home and hurried back to my own. I sat on the kitchen floor and hugged Flora. "We don't know how good we have it," I said. I opened the refrigerator door and eyed a pint of chocolate chip ice cream. But before a meeting could be called to order, I slammed the door shut. I would direct my anger at its source instead of burying it with food.

The following day Tiny and I returned to the "dog house" as I came to call it. For the next several days we did the same, passing it on the opposite side of the street. I wouldn't see the little girl, or her dog, until almost two weeks later.

She was sitting alone again on the front steps wearing the same dirty yellow dress. I was so excited to see her I didn't notice Tiny was pulling me over for another visit. He dragged me until my foot became twisted in a crack in the sidewalk. I fell to the ground. The huge mastiff continued without me on the other end of his leash. "Tiny," I screamed. "Come back."

Suddenly a wild man bolted from inside the house and rushed toward Tiny. He scooped up a large rock and threw it at the dog's back leg. His aim was good. Tiny yelped, baring his teeth. Rearing up on his haunches he pressed his full weight against the fence lunging for the man.

I limped over to Tiny, frantically pulling back on his leash.

The man backed off. "Get that stupid dog out of here!" he shouted. "People need to mind their own damn business."

I got control of Tiny and walked him away. "The dog isn't the stupid one," I yelled back at him over my shoulder.

On my way home palm trees swayed in an orange sky as another mid-July day came to an end. I sat down on a curb, picking tiny pebbles from my knee with a shaking hand. Tiny put his soggy muzzle in my lap. I stroked him between the eyes. My heart thumped so hard it felt like it would fall out of my chest.

I spoke out loud to steady myself. "That's the last person, or animal you'll ever bully, mister."

That night, I told my parents about everything.

"Why didn't you tell us sooner?" my mother asked. I sat at the dinner table, my sore ankle wrapped up and elevated.

I didn't have a good answer. Maybe I thought it really wasn't my business, or if I just kept an eye on the situation, things might be okay. But I also sensed that a little girl's life could be changed forever and that was a scary thought. I didn't want to be the one who caused any more trouble for her.

Later that evening, my father made some phone calls. He told me to stay away from that house. And I did.

'Family Removed from Home by Authorities...' the local newspaper headlines announced one week later. 'Abusive Breeder of Dogs Arrested...' declared another. The "dog house" was declared unfit for living. Family services had removed the little girl, and several crates filled with puppies and dogs were taken away by a division of animal control.

"Apparently they've been investigating those people for a while," my father explained. "Your involvement just sped up the process."

My relief was mixed with sadness. I wondered what would happen to all those animals and the little girl now. In a strange way, their sad situation had changed my life for the better. I'd walked off fifteen pounds and I'd learned that my troubles were pretty small compared to those of some others. And I'd come to see that I had the power to change my own situation; the how, where….and when. And the when was now.

"You dogs do a lot of good for a lot us humans," I said to Flora. "I'm sorry for the humans who just don't appreciate it."

From that point on, the only thing that was expanding in my life was my outlook, and my business. A collie, a pair of apricot poodles and several dogs of unknown origin soon joined my client list. That was good, because I needed the money. I was dropping pounds so fast I would have to buy a lot of new school clothes. And Flora needed a new collar or two. Her old one had grown too big and loose due to her own weight loss. It looked like she would be around for that extra year or so after all.

Labor Day and the start of a new school year would soon be here. But holidays and special dates were no longer my motivation for change. Life had gotten better for me and some others when my best friend, Flora, helped me to start losing the wait.

Human Directional

Enlightenment can be obtained in houses of worship, halls of education, on a magnificent mountain top, or sometimes in the confines of a sweaty dog suit working as a Human Directional.

Human Directionals. You've seen them, how could you not? Located at the busy intersections of cities and suburbs nation-wide, these living breathing human billboards, hoisting big signs shaped like arrows have become part of the American landscape. Some dance and jump around in staged excitement, swirling, swinging, flipping, and twirling their signs. Others stand slumped, stuck in place, brought down by boredom, heat, exhaustion…life.

But that sign they cling to is a life raft, offering its carrier a way to stay afloat during uncertain economic times. Signs eagerly pointing toward the Grand Opening of some new store in a strip mall, or directing house hunters to a housing tract that features mini-mansions listed at "Market Adjusted" prices.

Does anyone ever grow up wanting to be a Human Directional? Probably not. You'll find in most cases that these hired walking signs have surrendered hope, at a point in their lives when any job will do because they lack skills, accreditation, or opportunity. Many exist in quiet desperation looking for some personal direction, some kind of sign, while actually being one. Most won't get the irony, but there are exceptions, like John, a twenty-five year old college graduate with a degree in business from a prestigious university.

This formerly goal-directed young man had been laid off a year earlier and never did find something to replace that good run of employment he'd enjoyed for three years. Since then he'd done some light carpentry work, some house painting and worked as a busboy. He'd become discouraged about the prospects of ever finding meaningful work with a good salary, the kind of work he felt someone with his education and background deserved.

John recalled a time not so long ago when he held little regard for those who were not so smart, so lucky, so entitled; those individuals who labored on the lawns of others, waited on tables at chain restaurants, or flipped greasy burgers at fast-food joints. But now here he stood at a busy intersection dressed in a human-sized dog suit, luring customers to a store called PETS-4-U!

He had found his new job after answering an ad on Craig's List, under the heading of Advertising and Promotion. In desperate times the John's of the world overlook a lot, including their inner compasses, when accepting a position like that of a Human Directional for a place like PETS-4-U!

PETS-4-U! had been in business at its new spot for just four months, having moved from one a few miles down the road where it had been known as PUPS-2-GO! Now with the Thanksgiving and holiday season near, it was time to take advantage of this new highly trafficked business location and rev up the lucrative sale of adorable pups.

"I need someone with a big bark and lots of energy," the owner of the shop had explained to John during his interview. "If you can be available weekends, you're hired." he'd continued. "I'll start you out at $15.00 an hour and if business is good, I'll give you a raise and a holiday bonus."

As this was the best offer John had received in a while, he accepted. What more did he have to lose?

"Call me Ron," the pet shop owner had said offering John his hand. "Too bad those good looks of yours will be wasted." With this, he'd presented John with his new uniform, a Golden retriever suit which John would be wearing on his beat. "Get it? You're a member of the Working Dog Group now, a retriever of customers," Ron said, guffawing. "You can start tomorrow. Just keep that big arrow pointed in this direction and move around a lot, get creative, act like a dog, chase cars, offer your paw. Kids love it!"

John reported to his corner the next morning dressed in a dog suit the color of the amber-hued lagers he used to enjoy at the upscale bars he'd frequented after business hours in days of yore. He would have to get used to the stifling sensation that came with wearing a big dog head with slits for eyes, grateful it allowed him to remain anonymous.

The first hour passed without incident, but then it started. As a car idled at a red light, John twirled and flipped his sign at the woman in the driver's seat. "Moron," she yelled, flipping him the bird. "That place sells sick dogs from puppy mills. You should be ashamed of yourself."

But the SUV just behind her car, loaded with smiling kids brought better results. From the car, a small boy waved at him, "Yay! We're getting a dog," he screamed as the car pulled into the parking lot of the strip mall.

"Ca-ching," said John. He waved at the car offering the boy a two paws up sign.

John reported back to Ron after his first day of successfully directing humans to the store. "Good work, son," Ron said. "Lots of traffic today."

John removed his dog suit then took a good look around. Stacks of crates filled with puppies of all shapes, sizes and colors lined the walls. There must have been at least fifty. Some pups slept curled up in balls, others yelped and cried, sticking their little noses and paws through the bars of the crate as if begging for a loving touch. John placed his finger on the under pad of a poodle puppy's paw.

"Don't get too attached to the merchandise," Ron said.

"Where do all these puppies come from?"

Ron was careful in his response. "Commercial Breeders from all over the nation. That's all you need to know. Do a good job, and don't ask too many questions and ignore everyone's comments out there. Who knows? If you're looking for a new career direction, maybe I'll make you a sales associate. Good money in dogs."

Everyone's comments? John wondered, recalling the woman who'd called him a moron earlier in the day. How many other irate people would he have to deal with? John walked over to a crate with two yellow lab pups. "How much do you get for these guys?" he asked.

"Two grand apiece on a good day," Ron said, smiling. "Labs are my bread and butter. Everybody loves 'em. Can't get enough."

John gazed at the dozens of cages before him. "There are so many dogs here, what happens if you can't sell them all?"

Now Ron stood right in front of John, looking him directly in the eyes. "You're not one of those undercover animal activist-types are you, sent here to spy on me?"

John looked puzzled. Did people actually do that? He wondered. The only undercover work he was doing involved wearing a dog suit.

Nearby, an attractive young female employee was cleaning out a crate. She glanced quickly over at John and their boss as if tuned to their conversation. John smiled, thinking she might be checking him out. She did not respond in kind. Instead she quickly looked away as if to hide her face.

"See this guy right here?" Ron asked, now pointing to a Boxer pup. "He's getting a little too old so he's harder to sell. I'll start marking him down and see what I can get for him. When your mark-ups run around three-hundred percent, there's a lot of room to negotiate."

"What happens if he still doesn't sell?"

Ron sighed, signaling the conversation was about to end. "They have their place in this process. Some go back to the breeder and become breeding stock. Grist for the mill so to speak," he explained. "Just go out and do your job and then maybe we won't have to worry about any leftovers."

Ron was right. It really was none of his business. He was just a hired hand getting paid by the hour. He would keep his mouth shut and keep this job he so badly needed. Besides, there might be a new career opportunity here for him.

But the next day on the corner brought new troubles. A woman on foot came up to him and screamed right into his eye hole. "You're helping a bad man sell unhealthy pups!" As she walked off she yelled back at him. "We'll be back and we'll shut him down just like we shut down PUPS-2-GO!"

We? John thought, slightly alarmed. It was an unusually warm late-November day and with this exchange, John was now covered in sweat, wishing he could remove the head of the costume, but not daring to. He thought about the Boxer pup and other potential leftovers and with this he found new energy. If he hustled maybe he could get all of those dogs sold and into good homes. "Every dog has its day." He found some comfort in the old adage.

John relayed these threatening encounters to his boss at the end of his shift. "Occupational hazard," Ron replied. "There are a lot of crazies out there."

"They say that you're abusing dogs; that they're going to shut you down just like before. What does that mean?"

Ron stopped him. "Some people think they have the right to interfere with a man's right to free enterprise. Just ignore them. Remember, out there you're a dog, you have no voice."

The next few days went on with the usual mild heckling, but by the weekend the dog food really hit the fan. As John stood on his corner at High Noon, someone chucked an open can of wet dog food at him as they passed at a good clip. It hit his shoulder, or haunches, covering the dog suit with brown mush.

"Ah, crap," he muttered, cleaning himself up. When he looked up, the top of his dog head met with the clunk of a raw hide bone ejected from a passing car with the force of a rocket launch. That's when he noticed a small crowd of people moving toward him like a pack of wolves. Each clutched a wad of yellow flyers. The pack leader, with a microphone at his side, spoke to John.

"Look, I don't know you or why you're doing this, but I just thought I'd give you a heads up that we're here to stage a protest against the owner of that pet store you're promoting. We shut his business down last year, we can do it again."

John stood his ground. "What do you have against him? He's just trying to get by like all of us. What's wrong with selling dogs?"

"Do you know where those pups come from, really?" the megaphoned man asked.

"Breeders, they come from professional breeders," John answered, his voice strangely muffled by his costume, and growing guilt.

"They come from Commercial breeders, also known as puppy mills," the man answered. "The parents of those dogs live in horrible conditions, treated like garbage."

John countered. "Well, then isn't it a good thing that their pups will get good homes?"

"Many of those pups are sick and the people buying them don't even know it yet." The man answered. "Every time someone forks over cold cash to that guy, he goes out and buys more pups from those awful places and you're just helping him."

Grist for the mill... the words uttered by Ron the other day now took on a new meaning.

As much as he hated to admit it, John suspected the man was right. For the past few days, he had been doing a little research of his own about puppy mills, and about the business practices of his boss. The selling of dogs was a dirty business. At the start of the New Year, he would resign, no longer be a part of the problem.

But right now, he needed the money. Free enterprise, crazies, don't talk to them...Ron's words came back to him. John kept silent. Turning his hairy back on the crowd he resumed his work, hopping around in circles for a SUV filled with giggling kids.

But it wasn't so easy. The pack leader placed his hand on John's shoulder to stop him. John turned around to confront the man. "Keep your paws off me, man."

"Who wants a belly rub?" the man taunted John just before placing a well-placed punch to his abdomen area. But the dog suit had confused the man. Misjudging his aim, the punch was delivered to John's groin area.

John slumped down on the ground. "Shi...itzu," he cried, noticing a SUV filled with kids staring at him and crying in horror. They screamed out the back window of the car, "Mommy, someone's beating up a dog." In his pain, John picked up his sign and waved it in the air hoping to calm the distraught kids. But the vehicle headed away with the speed of a get-away car after a bank heist.

"That's just a little taste of what the parent's of those pups go through in their miserable lifetime," the man sneered as the rest of his pack pulled away from its prey and headed toward PETS-4-YOU!

The man placed a flyer in the paw of John's suit before rejoining them. For John this was overkill. He didn't need to read it to get the message that had already been so succinctly delivered.

Still not fully recovered John followed, unsteadily. The incident had shaken him and he needed time to think. But as he neared the store, the puncher who was just outside the shop's front window, turned abruptly to confront him again.

"Look, I don't want any more trouble," John said. But the guy grabbed John's arrow-shaped sign and started poking him with it. John tackled the man to the ground where they wrestled like two energetic pups, fighting over a squeaky toy. Now he was really earning his hourly wage as a Human Directional as people from all corners flocked toward the store.

Ron was in back of the shop waiting for a shipment of Chihuahuas from the Midwest when a customer finally alerted him to the show that was unfolding outside his front door. He ran outside trying to pull John off the protestor by the tail of his costume. When this failed, he grabbed his employee by the scruff of his costumed neck and hauled him inside the shop.

Without missing a beat, the protestor snatched up the microphone and led the crowd in chants of "Dog killer" and "Shut this place down now!" The crowd grew larger as more protestors arrived. Carrying their own signs, they had become Human Directionals of another sort.

"Are you insane?" Ron said when he'd gotten John back inside the store. From their crates, a litter of Cavalier King Charles spaniel pups started to whimper as if they smelled danger.

"Those people are really pissed. And maybe they have a right to be," John shot back still in costume, minus the head. His hair was wet and wild from his encounter, sticking up in all directions. It gave him the appearance of a mad man.

"The only right I care about is my right to be in business. You're fired. I'll pay you for today, but that's it. I should have known you were a sucker by all your stupid questions. This was a big mistake."

Ron walked to the back of the store where the dark-haired young woman John had seen the previous day, stood watching her boss's every move.

"Keep your money," said John, surprising even himself. "From what I can tell, it's blood money. It stinks of the smell of a million dead and dying dogs."

Ron shouted back. "Why don't you go join your new friends, then?"

The front door of the shop opened and a huge shadow fell over John.

"You the owner?" a man of about six foot four asked. He wore a large grey hooded jacket that looked to be concealing something.

John nodded a no. Not taking his eyes off the man, he pointed to the back of the shop.

"Yo. I want to talk to you man," he yelled. "Come on out here."

Ron stuck his head from out of the office. "What's the problem?" he asked.

"My wife came back here twice with vet bills for a sick puppy she bought a month ago," the man answered.

Ron came out of the office, cautiously making his way toward the front. "And?" he asked the man.

"That dog was sick and you knew it. You promised her you would pay all the vet bills, three thousand dollars worth," he confronted Ron.

Ron paused midway between the back exit and this man who was clearly becoming angrier by the moment. "But you didn't. You ignored her, didn't even return her calls," he continued. "That pup was a gift to my kid for her tenth birthday. I just got back from serving in the Mid-East. I don't need to deal with this crap, a crying wife and kid and...."

"I always offer to replace a sick dog with another. That's my policy."

"Policy?" The man sneered. "You can't replace a kid's pet like some stupid toy."

"Do you have the vet bills?" Ron asked, his voice now lacking its usual arrogance.

The man reached into his coat, "It's too late," he said.

With that Ron's face froze in horror while his feet turned toward the back. "Gun! He's got a gun, run!" he shouted. He fled out of the shop using the exit leading to the receiving area. The sound of the door slamming shut was obscured by the screeching of tires and a sickening thud followed by a series of shouts.

John turned to face the man, whose sad eyes met his. From under his coat he pulled the small body of a Chihuahua. At first John thought it was sleeping. "He knew it was sick," said the man. "I told my wife not to buy a pup at a pet store but my kid wanted one on her birthday. She didn't want to wait."

John stared at the small lifeless body of the puppy. He removed his dog suit and joined the girl in the back. She was looking out the window of the door at a large van in the shipment area.

"There's nothing we can do. In dog-speak we would say Ron has gone to the Rainbow Bridge," she said. "But even if he was allowed to cross, he would be in for a big surprise."

"What's the Rainbow Bridge?" John asked.

She explained that it was a place where dogs and their loving owners were reunited in heaven. Then she told John that she'd been doing undercover work for an animal advocacy group that had been working to shut down Ron's store. John recalled her secretive behavior from the other day.

"We have time to get some of these pups out of here," she spoke. From the office, she disabled the video surveillance system, removed the tape and quickly began opening crates.

John walked to the front of the store where the grieving man stood, still staring at the dead puppy on the counter. Going over to the crate of the aging Boxer pup, John removed it and handed it to the man. "Take this dog. Go out the back door. There's an angry mob out front."

The man looked at John questioningly. "He's getting too old to sell and I don't know what will happen to him. Maybe he's in better health than that poor Chihuahua."

The sounds of an ambulance approached as John escorted the man out of the store. Just steps away a distracted crowd hovered over the unmoving body of the store owner.

"I didn't see him," the apparent driver of a delivery truck kept repeating. "He just shot out in front of me. I didn't have a chance to stop."

John looked at a large vehicle that idled nearby. From inside the distressed yips of nervous young pups cried out. It was the delivery Ron had been waiting for, the delivery that would be his last.

"Well, are you going to help me or not?" the dark haired girl called back to John. "This is your chance to make up for all the bad you've done this week."

She was right. He couldn't just walk away. Maybe he couldn't change the circumstances in his own life right now, but he could help change the fates of some unfortunate dogs. In that realization his life took on a new direction, one fueled by a sense of purpose that had been lacking in him for so long. Maybe every dog couldn't have its day, but he could see to it that some could. He began emancipating pups, scooping up several at a time, bringing them out through the front entrance.

John walked over to the group of protestors who were not yet aware of his boss's demise. He spoke to the man who had attacked him previously, "Looks like this shop has shut itself down for a while." The crowd grew quiet. "There are a lot of pups in there," John continued to address them.

"We'll take what we can now and then we'll try and rescue the rest later."

"We'll all get thrown in jail for theft," someone said.

John shrugged. "But we'll be letting some innocent prisoners out," he answered. "Time's a' wasting, let's go." With that directive, he ran back into the store.

Maybe stealing these pups was breaking the law of man, but certainly in this case, not the law of a higher power he reasoned. He had no choice; it felt good to be a hero for a change.

He had become a Human Directional in the very best sense of the word.

Stipend of a Sucker

A stipend is defined as a type of payment for an intern or an apprentice that is sometimes complimented with other perks such as food and lodging; a sucker is someone who is easily duped or deceived. A sucker can actually be on the giving or receiving end of a stipend depending on how you look at it; figuring out on which end of the sucker equation one falls is sometimes tricky.

But recently, during a visit to my therapist, I found it wasn't so tricky after all. There, I'd come to the painful realization I was indeed a chronic sucker; on the losing end of things in most of my personal arrangements.

On my eighth session, my therapist, Dr. Althea Wolfe, had inquired, "So, have you ever figured out just how much each bad relationship in your life has cost you?"

"What do you mean?" I'd replied. "Like in money?"

With her question, I sank back into the worn leather of an oversized armchair, seeking comfort and distance in its depth. She leaned forward, hands placed firmly on her lap, poised to deliver an insight like the beacon of a lighthouse guiding a lost ship through unchartered waters.

Dr. Wolfe continued; her probing brown eyes fixed on me. "You say that you find yourself always reaching for your purse whenever someone close to you needs a "loan" (she did that air thing with her fingers) or some kind of well, for lack of better words, a stipend."

We had been talking about my current relationship with my boyfriend, Roger, another pairing that was entering the make it or break it stage at the one year mark. I knew I'd lost time with my poor choices of companions, but in terms of lost money I really hadn't a clue.

Her question had conjured up images that whirled through my head like a psychic storm; there I was whipping out a credit card, checkbook, or a wad of cold hard cash, doling out funds usually in amounts disproportionate to the "services" or affection rendered in return. And yes, food and lodging was often involved, too.

I knew where Dr. Wolfe was going with this; I'd become a pushover, an enabler, a sucker. "So," she pressed for an answer, "have you ever thought about the link between your allotment of funds and your relationships?"

From downstairs, the smell of greasy eggrolls from the busy kitchen of a Chinese restaurant wafted through the open window of the office. It mingled with the wail of a car alarm and the howling of a dog, a sensory overload that jarred me out of my trance. I squirmed in my chair and then leaned forward for a meeting of the minds; eyes locked with my therapist who sensed correctly that her patient was finally on the brink of self-revelation.

"Have you ever sat down and figured out the average dollar amount you've invested in a relationship by the time you've figured out that things weren't working out?" she asked again as if I wasn't able to grasp the concept. But I was. It was just taking time to sink in.

She didn't press for an answer, she had made her point. Looking at her watch she stood up and announced, "Our session is over. We'll continue with this next time. When you're up to it, go over your bank and credit card statements from the last seven years and look for a pattern."

My mind had become a calculator; so distracted by my thoughts laced with numerical facts and figures, I'd gathered up my things and started to walk out the door without paying. "Um, I know I suggested you stop being a sucker," she said, "But hopefully you think my advice is still worth a stipend."

"Sorry. Your question kind of got me worked up."

"That's a good thing," she said smiling as I handed her a check.

Back on the street I slipped into a diner and ordered a latte and called my friend, Christina.

"A stipend?" she'd asked, hooting with laughter. "But seriously, she's right and you know it. You just can't say no. People always take advantage of your good nature. Why are you paying an expensive therapist? I've been telling you this free-of-charge for years now."

Christina was a professional dog obedience trainer. Sometimes her approach to life was infuriatingly simple. "The key to happiness can be found in the commands of "Sit, Stay, Heel," she liked to proclaim. In her world, the principles of dog obedience could be applied to most any human situation.

I defended myself. "Well, sometimes people are in a tough spot. They need a little help to get by." I already knew what kind of reaction this would get.

"Yes, but they "get by," and then say "good-bye," and who's always on the losing end?" she asked. "They've trained you to give them everything they need. Walk, treat, belly rub, pick up restaurant tab, make car payment, forgive credit card dept, post bail, and then they turn around and bite you in the ass."

"Hey!" I protested.

"I just threw the bail and bite thing in there for added effect," Christina said laughing. "But you know it's true. What are you getting out of all of this? I say dump that leech of a boyfriend and just go out and get a dog. If you're going to be a rescuer, you may as well reap the rewards of your kindness. Oh, and then you can hire me as a trainer of course."

"Thanks. I'll put that on the list of things to ponder," I replied taking the last long sip of my latte.

Christina said she had to run. Her Saturday afternoon was filled with appointments with the owner of a Keeshond that kept attacking its own shadow, a new client with a freshly adopted pit bull mix, and a Chocolate lab with severe separation anxiety issues.

"See if you break up with Roger, I can even help you with your separation anxiety. I'll even give you a "Two for One Discount," she said before hanging up.

I wandered back toward home. Stopping at a crosswalk, I looked down into the eyes of a little French bulldog standing at attention next to its owner. Having a dog trainer for a friend had taught me to identify breeds. Its intelligent black face with its piercing eyes and bat-like ears stared back up at me. He held his head cocked to one side as if reading my thoughts and if he could speak, he probably would've told me to get a dog, too.

Returning to my condo, I went directly to my files. At age thirty, I had a lot of material to go through, literally and figuratively. With the opening of each physical file, another one of a very different nature was accessed in my mind, complete with memories and emotion.

There was my college boyfriend who stepped right into graduate school. For two years, I had typed his papers, schlepped his laundry, shopped and cooked for him so he could concentrate on his studies. We both maintained jobs, his part-time, but my job as an administrative assistant at a law firm had covered most of our expenses. When he'd achieved his MBA, he'd taken up with an attractive female fellow business school grad.

"Hmmm...wonder what that experience cost me?" I said out loud, tapping on a calculator. "Five thou...sounds 'bout right." I made a note of it.

Soon after, an old college roommate from out of town had come knocking at my door.

"Hey," Carla had said on the phone after she had tracked me down four years after graduation. "I'm hoping to settle in this city. Why don't I stay with you? We can share expenses while I look for a job?"

Her definition of "share" was interesting. By the end of four months, despite her "best" efforts, she still hadn't found a job worthy of her background, talents and education. By the time she had moved on and in with a guy she had met at a club, I was a loser on this end of that deal, too. She had barely coughed up any money for rent, food or utilities, and I later discovered she had exited with a pair of expensive Italian boots she had "borrowed," a box full of CDs and a cashmere sweater. I low-balled my loss for her at about one-thousand dollars.

Then, out of the blue, a young male cousin had appeared on my doorstep looking for a temporary place to get his act together. Charming and fun to be around, Kevin was a recently divorced jazz musician and house-painter who needed a place to "flop."

Kevin was so easy to have around I hardly noticed that three months of couch flopping had passed with only an occasional offer to cook dinner (with ingredients I purchased), some demo CDs and free admission to the clubs where he played his occasional gigs. I helped him find a permanent place to live before he was able to paint my living room like he'd promised in return for my generosity. I put him down for five hundred dollars in the debit column.

Throughout the years there had been assorted needy boyfriends. Like Tom, who needed new brakes for his truck, one-thousand bucks worth, and Stephen's stipend of five-hundred dollars to help him get his Personal Trainer Certificate. He'd taken up with a yoga instructor upon receiving his credentials compliments; of me. Now there was Roger, my current intern, who at this time was in need of a new computer and scanner for his budding graphics business. Who knew what that would cost?

All told, the average amount of money I had spent "helping" others rang in around one-thousand and six hundred dollars per episode, or apprentice. Voila, so there it was; my stipend fully flushed out for my unflinching consideration.

I had reasoned that I enjoyed a nice life-style afforded by my challenging but meaningful career as a Senior Vice President of Marketing at a large entertainment company. What was so wrong about helping others if it made me happy?

But did it?

I knew then what my therapist was asking me to confront. My habit of being a sucker was taking its toll on my too-generous soul. No one liked to be exploited. It was self-denial that kept me from asking the universe to make me the center of someone else's world for a change, to reap the benefits of a divine reciprocity, where you got as good as you received.

My cell rang. It was Roger.

"What's the matter? He asked as if sensing my mood. "You sound funny."

"Nothing, really," I lied. "I'm just going over some figures, trying to balance things."

Roger laughed. "Yeah, that can be a bitch for sure." I noted his interesting choice of that word; curiously it brought to mind a female dog. We made quick plans to meet and travel uptown to a street fair.

Once there, amongst the scents of the festival food court, colorful art displays and the distractions of the loud crowded city street, I found my mood improving. We stopped to order some gyros from a Greek food vendor's booth, purchased by me of course, and sat down curbside to eat.

Directly across from me under a big canopy, a local animal shelter had set up house, complete with some adorable dogs available for adoption. I couldn't take my gaze off a shaggy medium-sized dog, its eyes trying to focus on me through the passing legs of humans that obscured his view. Roger was saying something, but I was no longer listening.

Get a dog…Christina's words came back to me.

"Hey, are you hearing anything I'm saying?" Roger asked. "So like I was saying,"
he continued before I could answer. "If I could just borrow about one-thousand and five hundred bucks, or so, I could get that scanner I told you about. What do you say?"

One-thousand five-hundred dollars… it was close enough to make a point. My sucker days were over.

"I say that I'll be right back," was my reply.

I walked back over to the adoption booth and asked if I could meet the medium-sized grey and brown dog with one white paw. A young girl led me into a gated pen and introduced us. The dog greeted me like an old friend. I don't know how long I spent with her; time seemed to stop as the shelter volunteer spoke to me.

"She's an older dog," the girl explained, speaking fast and deliberately, honestly presenting the dog while making her appealing as possible. "She was just transported from a Shelter in Mississippi so we named her Dixie. Looks to be some kind of terrier mix, maybe about five or six…."

"I'll take her," I said, cutting her off. "What do I have to do?"

The girl stopped talking and smiled, looking relieved. "Thank you. Sometimes it's hard to place an older dog; everyone seems to want a puppy. You'll just have to fill out some paper work, and then there's a two-hundred and fifty dollar adoption fee."

Taking all the papers and information from her I returned to Roger. Sitting back down on the curb I dealt with the forms and then I took out my check book and wrote a check in the amount of one-thousand and seven-hundred and fifty dollars, payable to the rescue organization.

Poor Roger misunderstood my gesture.

"Thanks, babe. You're a life saver," he said.

"Yes, I guess you could say that. But this isn't for you."

Roger looked perplexed. "What's that check for then?"

"Well, you want fifteen hundred, and the adoption fee is two-hundred and fifty dollars. That's my stipend, but this time it's the stipend of a sucker who can't refuse a furry face."

A look of confusion spread across his face. "Stipend?" he asked. "Furry face?" He stroked the dark stubble on his chin as if feeling for fur. "Sucker?"

I told Roger I had another engagement. "I'll call you," I said, walking back over to the rescue booth.

"Son of a bitch," I heard him say.

See, there's that word again…

Back at the booth, I handed in my papers and the check and made arrangements to be available the next day. I hurried away before they could discover the amount of their "stipend."

With a lighter heart and new energy, I headed toward a large pet supply shop. Like a kid in a toy store, I explored each aisle for leashes, collars, squeaky toys and treats. There was nothing my new dog would want for.

Yes, I was still a sucker. But I knew this time my kindness and generosity would be appreciated, and that in fact, Dixie would probably be the sucker in this deal. For I knew already that no stipend offered by me in the form of food, shelter or love could ever be enough to repay her for what she would surely do for me.

I looked forward to my next session with Dr. Wolfe. Somehow I knew it would probably be my last.

La Casa del Feliz Perro

The House of the Happy Dog

"Buenos dias, Mr. Thomas. Will you be joining us for breakfast?" Oscar, a short stocky man with jet-black hair inquired of me. I'd just stepped onto the porch of the small inn where I'd been staying for the past seven-days. My vacation had come to an end and this morning's meal would be my last at this charming Mexican establishment.

"Si, I'll have breakfast or should I say desayuno?" I replied, showing off my expanding Spanish vocabulary. I took a seat at my regular table set with a crisp white linen cloth, sapphire blue napkins, and the colorful pottery made by locals. A ceiling fan whirred directly above me; at eight o'clock it was already a scorcher.

The efficient Oscar poured my coffee. "The usual, huevos y frijoles, eggs and black beans?" he asked with a warm familiarity. During my brief stay here Oscar and I had enjoyed a good-natured battle of the languages, the stubborn Mexican had been as eager to practice his English as I'd my Spanish. We'd settled into a casual mix of both.

Oscar ran back into the small inn to help his wife, Concetta, fix my farewell meal. For the past several years the couple had helped run this place for an absentee owner.

Located just a few miles south of Playa del Carmen, I'd discovered this little gem of a hideaway while looking for a much-needed winter getaway.

Divorced two years earlier, it had been difficult to plan a vacation for one at age sixty. The prospect of traveling alone was formidable and I'd found myself putting it off. My search for the perfect vacation spot had been exhaustive and confusing with too many choices. Then I'd found it, a place that called to me.

It hadn't been the images on the inn's web page. Its promotional photos were typical of most resorts; images of impossibly white sandy beaches, bordered by lush green tropical landscapes and an unbelievably blue-green sea. No, it was the inn's name that had sealed the deal, La Casa del Perro Feliz which in English translates to the House of the Happy Dog. In my mind, any place that suited a happy dog was a good enough place for me.

But on my first day at the inn, I had been disappointed when no dog greeted me as I checked in at the front desk.

"No. perro, no esta aqui," Oscar had explained to me when I inquired about the dog. "No dogs here anymore," he repeated in English, a sad shadow briefly crossing his cheerful face. He picked up my suitcase and led me to my room on the second floor. "Settle in, I will have my wife prepare almuerzo, lunch, for you." I wanted to ask what happened to the dog, but decided to save that question for another time.

That opportunity presented itself while I dined on the inn's porch the following morning. A scattering of dark clouds temporarily hid the sun as rain from a passing cloudburst pinged loudly on the house's orange-tiled roof. From the depth of the surrounding forest, howler monkeys screeched among a leafy canopy of treetops while parrot-like birds squawked in return.

"Mas café?" Oscar offered.

"No, Oscar. No more coffee gracias, pero, I have una pregunta," I struggled with my butchered Spanish.

"Si, yes," Oscar nodded. "What is your question?"

"Donde esta the dog, el perro ahora?" I inquired about the current whereabouts of the happy namesake of the inn.

Oscar nodded sadly. "Muerto. Dead. Dos, two years ago. Mr. Evans, the boss of this place and owner of el pero, go home to California. Don't come back much anymore."

Leaving my table to service another guest, Oscar left me alone with my Mexican omelet and my thoughts. Then I'd noticed a wooden hand-painted sign hanging above the inn's front door. It bore the faded image of a large black dog curled up in a siesta. I clearly pictured this dog napping in the shady corner of the porch, or begging for food from the guests. I found it odd how an animal I had never even met intrigued me and would continue to do so throughout my stay.

During my last morning meal a rustling in a small stand of palmettos caught my attention. Barefooted, I stepped off the porch sinking into the warm sand and headed down the path toward the ocean. Just a few yards away from the inn, I spotted the tip of a snout and two beady eyes peering from behind some vegetation. Cautiously one small dog approached, followed by another; their tails wagged in unison as they neared, noses pointed upward in the air toward the House of the Happy Dog.

"Are we hungry?" I asked the one that looked like a mix of Chihuahua and poodle. "Wait here. I'll see what I can do."

Back up on the porch, Oscar caught me stealthily wrapping the remains of my breakfast in a napkin. I told him about the dogs, but his response to my attempt to feed them perplexed me. "No. Do not invite them aqui!"

"Por que. Why?" I implored.

"They are too many dogs starting to come here now. Mucho perros. And if you feed beans they will, how you say, steenk?" Oscar replied, his lips curled in disgust as he fanned the air. Es malo, very bad! The guests they do not like."

"But why don't you give one of those dogs a home and make it happy?" I asked. "It could be the nuevo perro, the new dog that makes the house happy."

Oscar nodded his head deliberately. "No sir, Mister Evan's dog was very special. Not just any dog can come and, how you say, replace. Has to be muy especial!"

Dejected, I trashed my leftovers and sat down on the inn's front steps. I gazed in the direction where I had last seen the strays. Back home, these dogs might be considered an expensive hybrid with a made-up name like a Chichipoo, or a Poo-wawa, but here they were just plain old unwanted Mexican mutts.

I tossed a small piece of banana toward an iguana sunning itself on a large rock. After a moment it sprung into action, swallowing the treat whole with two gulps. At least I can feed the reptiles, no gassy issues there, I thought.

I looked down at the tops of my sunburned sand-encrusted feet, thinking about the past dogs in my life, wondering why I had remained without one for so long.

Somewhere in my attic back home there was an old beat up trunk containing some of my favorite boyhood photos that captured the images of me and the family dog of the moment. My personal favorite; a picture of me holding a beagle bassett hound mix named Long Shot.

In that grainy black and white snapshot with its wavy white border, my arms are wrapped around the dog, his gangly body pinned vertically down the front of the flannel shirt I practically lived in at the time. The dog's hindquarters dangle almost to the floor, his nose pressed under my chin. Across my goofy ten-year old face is a look of pure happiness.

When Long Shot died two years after that picture was taken I was inconsolable, sitting and sobbing for hours on the curb outside my house until I threw-up just yards from the wheels of the neighbor's truck that had taken my dog's life.

A few days after my loss, the German shepherd that lived across the street had given birth to eight pups. "Would Thomas like a pup?" I heard her ask my mother one evening. But I'd dramatically declined that offer; declaring there could never be a replacement for my lost best friend.

"Buck up son," my dad advised. "Dogs come and dogs go. This time we'll get a leash and build a fence."

His mater-of-fact approach had angered me. I loved Long Shot and felt responsible for his death for not having watched over him more carefully. But eight weeks later, when my mother presented me with a cuddly pup from our neighbor's litter, I had experienced a change of heart.

If you dig deeper in that box of old photos in my attic, you'll find several of me with my arms around a giant black German shepherd dog named Shadow. The year is 1960, my hair is full and long and the flannel shirt has been replaced by one that's tie-dyed. I am leaving home and my dog, to go off to college. I am smiling with excitement, anticipating my freedom, but if you look closely, Shadow and I look a little sad.

I remember trying to explain to the goofy guy that I would be back, but he gave me a look that said, "You chose me, you promised to be there for me and now you're abandoning me." He was right. Shadow died four years later, just weeks before I graduated and returned home.

Maybe that's why I hadn't allowed room for a canine in my life and my heart for so long. I just wasn't worthy. My ex-wife hadn't encouraged dog ownership; they were too dirty, too much responsibility, plus my kids had never even asked for one.

And there on the steps of La Casa del Perro Feliz I was stricken with a full-blown case of dog fever. A yearning that had remained dormant for decades now spread through my soul. When I got back to the States, I would join the army of seventy million dog owning American households. I would go to a shelter and find the remedy for my dog fever, a real butt sniffing, poop eating, squirrel chasing, slobbering, drinkin' out of the toilet bowl friend!

Maybe three would turn out to be the charm, I thought.

I looked at my watch; it was time to leave this paradise. I brushed the sand off my feet and waved my good-bye to the ocean. Oscar stood on the porch with my luggage as the shuttle van to the airport pulled up. "Gracias, amigo. Thanks for everything," I said to him. "I hope you find the right dog for your house someday."

"Yo espero tambien, Mr. Tom," he replied that he hoped so, too. "Someone once say to me that some dogs go through quatro casas, four houses, before getting to their true home, la casa verdad."

"That's a lot of homes. But, a lucky dog would be very happy to call this place his fourth and final one," I said. "And I think it would make the house's master happy again, too."

~

Somewhere in northern Florida, near an exit on Interstate 95, a towering sign offers weary sunburned tourists their last chance to purchase stale pecans and over-ripe citrus products before heading north. It's also the same exit one takes to get to the Giant Flea Market in Palatka.

The flea market consists of a caravan of huge tents separated by yards of dry dusty soil on sunny hot days, or slimy silt during the rainy spells. In these tents you can buy almost anything from ammo, bungee cords, knock-off sunglasses, gold by the yard, patio furniture, and even puppies.

And that is where a puppy named Simon, as I would come to call him, found his first family. A product of a puppy mill somewhere in the mid-west, Simon had been acquired at auction and now found himself for sale at the Palatka Pure-Bred Puppy Palace.

On this cloudy and humid Sunday in late March, Carlos Castillo, the proprietor of the family-owned puppy operation was on high alert. It was peak tourist season and the crowds at the market were strong with young spring-breaking families. He could count on the appearance of spoiled kids, returning home from their vacations already forgetting about their favorite theme park characters. Their nonstop cries for a puppy could wear down most any parent until they gave in.

Carlos could almost guarantee his crates of adorable puppies would draw a crowd. The tricky part was to make them irresistible, a skill he had developed to perfection.

On this day, Ledford Langston III, his wife Lavinia and their three young children were on their way home from Orlando when they decided to stop at the flea market.

For Ledford, it had been a miserable trip to the theme park; lots of rain, unbearable humidity and long lines for all the attractions. On the first and only sunny day of his vacation, Ledford, fair and redheaded, had fallen asleep floating on a raft in the hotel's pool. Having neglected to use sunscreen he'd been in pain ever since. At the moment, the Ledford children, Damien, Crystal, and Ashlee, were as cranky as their father.

While Ledford checked out rifles and hunting supplies, Lavinia draped long ropes of gold chain between her freshly polished fingers nails adorned with palm trees with tiny coconuts made with cubic zirconium. And just like Carlos had predicted the bored Langford children were cooperating with his plan, entertaining themselves by peering in the windows of his puppy shop.

Carlos could smell a sucker a mile away and from inside his store he sensed a high reading on his sucker-o-meter. He quickly retrieved his sales weapon of choice, a cuddly pup with black velvet fur that was nearing the four-month old mark. He went to work on the little Langstons, casually sauntering out to the front of his shop where the youngsters took one look at the adorable puppy and squealed with delight.

"Can I hold him?" begged nine-year-old Ashlee.

Carlos placed the pup in the girl's arms where it wasted no time trying to lick off her face.

"Ah, he likes you," Carlos cooed. "He doesn't like everyone."

His timing was perfect. The Langston parents were heading his way; now it was time for the hard sell.

"Whatcha' got there, kids?" Ledford asked.

"Look Daddy," eleven-year old Crystal said. "He's so cute, can we buy him?"

This was music to Carlos's ears. "You are in luck today, sir," he began. "We are having an Easter special this weekend. This particular puppy is on sale."

Unbeknownst to Carlos, Ledford had been contemplating a new hunting dog, perhaps a retriever or a hound. But certainly not this thing that looked like a mutant poodle.

By this time, the dog had migrated to the arms of Lavinia, working its magic. "What brand of dog is this?" she inquired.

Carlos did not answer her directly; he needed to plan his strategy. With her use of the word "brand," in place of breed, he appeared to be dealing with dog-ignorant people and he could use this to his advantage. Carlos had learned that certain pups could be passed off as other breeds while they were still young. Want a small cuddly lap dog? It was a Havanese or Cocapoo. Need a mid-size, water-loving canine? It became a Portuguese water dog. Was a larger dog more to your liking, then how about a Newfoundland or a Bouvier des Flandres?

Which this pup actually happened to be.

Carlos was acutely aware that this dog was growing rapidly and would soon be too big to pass off as a smaller breed, making him hard to sell. He had to unload this merchandise and do it quickly.

"Well, what brand of dog are you looking for?" Carlos asked.

"This kind," answered Ashlee.

Now Carlos addressed Ledford, going in for the hard sell. "You look like an active person, maybe a big sportsman. This dog could make a very good hunting partner for you."

"How big will it get?" Lavinia interrupted.

"Are you looking for a big dog?" Carlos said.

Lavinia nodded. "Oh no, not too big."

Ledford looked at his wife. "I don't want some small sissy dog."

Carlos prevailed. "Are you a boater sir?"

"Yeah, boatin's pretty cool. I got a nice little twenty-eight foot cabin cruiser back home near Savannah."

"Ah," Carlos replied, pushing his thick dark hair from his forehead, playing up his deep blue eyes and high cheekbones. He flashed a perfect white smile at Lavinia, a move that had sealed many a deal. "Then this is the perfect dog for you. It's a Portuguese water dog."

"Whoa!" Ledford responded. "A Porch-a-geese whoosie whater? Never heard of 'em."

"Well then my friend," said Carlos, "this is your lucky day. They are very rare indeed and he's the only one left in the whole place. I can make you a very nice deal."

Sitting on the ground below them little Ashlee tightened her grip around the pup's body, looking up at her dad. Outside the sun had returned full strength beating down on the market's tent tops, turning the place into one huge sauna. Ledford's face glowed bright red; sweat oozing from each pore. To make matters worse, or better for Carlos, Ashlee began to cry.

Ledford motioned for Carlos to walk back into the shop with him.

"How much money are we talkin'?" Ledford inquired. "I maxxed out my damn Visa card this week!"

"For you, sir, I can do seven hundred and fifty. I'll throw in a leash and a dog crate."

"How about seven, cash," Ledford countered.

"Sold!" Carlos proclaimed victoriously.

Ledford counted out seven crisp one hundred dollar bills, handing them to a beaming Carlos. He didn't even question why the man had given him such a strong leash with such a large collar; it was free after all.

Carlos watched the hapless new dog owners walk off with their new family member. Lavinia looked back, flashing him a big smile. The deal had gone down quicker than the express line for a popular water-ride on a hot day at one of those crowded tourist attractions. By the time the dog had grown, the Langstons would be too far away and the bonding with the dog too great for them to exchange the giant pooch for a different brand, or one in better health, perhaps.

But Carlos did not relax with this success. He shoved the wad of cash into his money pouch, eyeing the crowd for his next victim. A college-aged couple, wearing little more than beach clothes, was ogling a yellow lab pup in the shop's window. God how he loved those labs, they really knew how to attract a crowd and they were so easy to sell.

By the time they'd reached the Georgia border the Langston children had moved on with their wants. At this particular moment, they wanted lunch and demanded that Ledford and Lavinia pull into the parking lot of a Cracker Barrel Restaurant.

"Who's gonna stay in the car with this damn dog?" Ledford inquired. But before he finished the question the answer was clear. He was.

"I'll get you something to go, sweetie," Lavinia offered.

Ledford sighed and cranked up the AC. He stared stonily towards the dozing black ball of fur. "You're a big problem already," he spoke to the sleeping pup.

But Ledford had no idea just how big a problem he would soon have on his hands.

~

Upon my return home from Mexico, my dog fever had subsided just a little. Getting back to my daily routine of opening mail, returning phone calls, etcetera had absorbed some of its intensity.

But come nightfall it was a different story. Sipping margaritas, I found myself pouring over pictures of adoptable dogs on Petfinders.com and classified ads in the local paper. Each evening, before going to bed, I'd convince myself that I'd found just the right dog. Just before sleep found me, I'd promise myself I would call the shelter or a breeder the very next morning.

But come morning, I'd find myself sober and uncertain, beginning the entire process all over again 'round about mid-night. This cycle went on for a couple of weeks until fate brought me into the world of the Langston family.

In my retirement I had become a house painter. Outside of Savannah, homes had sprung up all over the place and I never lacked for work. On one hot late-August day, I found myself summoned to the home of Ledford Langston to give an estimate for a big painting job. I met Ledford for the first time outside his sprawling five-bedroom home that sat on a lawn that probably took a half-day to mow.

Life had been good to Ledford, as he told it. He and his brother had found success in the home spa and pool business. Then Ledford had branched out into the fake palm tree business, his words. He explained how even some restaurants way up in cold places like Michigan and Minnesota ordered his phony trees to provide a tropical atmosphere for their winter-weary customers. "It's easy to feel good around palm trees, even if their fake," he had explained.

But the economy had grown weak and so had Ledford's phony tree business.

"Yeah," No expensive vacations next year," Ledford explained to me as we walked the property. "I can barely afford to keep this place fixed up right." I knew he said this to influence my estimate.

But I'd stopped listening to the man's drivel by the time we'd gotten to the backyard. Something that resembled a pony was galloping full speed directly toward me. Through the air it sailed, knocking me down, licking me excitedly.

"No Bear!" yelled Ledford. He tugged at the giant dog's collar with all his strength. "I swear this dog weighs at least a ton."

"It's okay," I said. And it really was for at that moment I felt a joy I hadn't felt in years. Rolling from underneath this magnificent animal, I stood up just as Ledford smacked the dog on the backside and ordered him away.

"Portuguese water dog my butt," Ledford mumbled.

No way, I agreed silently. I knew dogs well enough to know that this doggy was a purebred Bouvier des Flandres, although the dog's ears and tail had not been docked.

"More like a pain in my neck is what he is," Ledford said dismissively. "I got him for the kids down at a flea market in Florida. They begged me to buy him and now they don't even give him the time of day. And my wife, she's just about had it with him."

I was going to explain to the man that the Bouvier was a special breed originally from Belgium and that the French had used them as guard dogs and sometimes for herding. But I knew that this knowledge would be wasted on him and at that moment, I was busy hatching a plan that involved me becoming the new "owner" of this glorious canine.

Now inside the Langston home, our footsteps echoed off bare walls as Ledford and I walked down the hardwood corridors of the mini-mansion. Ledford got right to the point. He needed two bedrooms and his living room painted and he was hurting for money.

"This lousy economy is ruining my palm tree enterprise," he ranted again. Apparently, the only thing selling these days were replacement parts for rusted and damaged metal palm fronds.

Upstairs in Crystal's room I was greeted with a page right out of The Little Mermaid. Hues of sea greens and watery blues covered the expansive room. "Crystal says she's tired of her bedroom, wants purple walls and Anna Dakota or Hanna Nevada stuff, whatever her name is, now," Ledford explained. "Kids today; so superficial."

Go figure. From outside the bedroom window, I kept my eyes on the big black dog sitting alone and bored in the middle of Ledford's enormous backyard with its swimming pool, complete with phony palm trees and a flashy waterfall. When Ledford was done airing his litany of problems, I gave him an estimate he couldn't turn down.

I got to work the very next day arriving at the Langston home with my ladder, drop cloths, rollers and hidden stash of dog treats. I would take my time on this project, as I was not being paid by the hour, but by the job. Who knew how long it would take?

By the time I prepped the room and began spreading a coat of Purple Crocus on the freshly primed walls of Crystal Langston's bedroom wall, I had bonded with Bear, privately renaming him Simon.

At lunch I'd sit in the shade of the Langston's canopied deck, resisting Lavinia's invitation to come into the house to enjoy the central air conditioning. Not without my friend I'd wanted to say. Refreshing his water dish frequently, Simon would thank me with a lick so wet I needed to towel dry my face. On days that were especially hot I would hose him down like a horse.

On day seven I was almost done painting Ashlee's room when I'd determined that the walls would require two coats of paint.

"Geez, how much extra's that gonna' cost me?" Ledford whined when I gave him the news. We'd been talking in the hallway outside Ashlee's room when the big dog made a fateful move. Somehow he had found a way to fully open the screen door in the kitchen. Once inside the house, he scrambled up the stairway bounding down the hall right toward us.

"Bear, no!" shouted Ledford. But within seconds the dog was romping around Ashlee's empty room, dipping his giant shaggy tail into an open bucket of "Lavender Lace" semi-gloss paint. Exiting the room the dog made his mark all the way down the ivory colored walls of the hallway, creatively adding his lavender accents with every swish of his tail.

"How much are you paying him?" I joked.

By now Ledford's face was completely crimson. He sputtered expletives in the dog's direction. I tried hard not to laugh, wondering if Ledford might have a heart attack, but in this seemingly disastrous scenario I saw a way to make everyone happy.

"Ledford," I said, commandingly. "Calm down."

The dog had stopped at the end of the hallway, staring in my direction. I grabbed a clean towel and stooped down. "Here boy," I said, calmly. The big dope sauntered over to me, his tail still full of paint. When he got to me I wrapped him in the towel and spoke to Ledford. "I'm going to take him into the bathtub and rinse him off. Follow me."

In the tub as I ran warm water over Simon's tail, I made my move. "Ledford, what you have here is a Bouvier de Flanders. A big dog now and he's not even full-grown yet."

"No sir," countered the man. "That's a Porchageeze water dog!"

"Ledford, let me ask you a few questions," I started. "Does this dog ever even attempt to take a swim in your pool out there?"

Ledford nodded a silent no.

"Look at his paws," I continued. "A Portie has webbed feet. I don't see any webbing in these babies." I held up one of the dog's giant paws for his inspection. "This is a breed for herding things, but not in the water."

"The only thing that dog herds is food into its gullet," Ledford said, moodily. "Damn thing's a windbag, too."

I made my move. "Let me take this dog off your hands. I can give him the home he needs."

Ledford nodded. "That dog, whatever brand you say it is, cost me a lot of money. I can't just give it to you!"

Obviously, the only thing that concerned the man was the dog's monetary worth.

"I'll paint your entire upstairs hallway, and the girls' bathroom in exchange for him."

Bingo! I had spoken Ledford's language. After a brief discussion and a handwritten amendment to my painting contract, the deal was done. At the end of the job, Simon would go home with me. I worked so fast I was finished in two days.

I don't know what Ledford planned to tell his kids, but on the final day on the job, after I'd cleaned up and packed the truck my only concern was for the dog. Ashlee, Crystal and Damien had their chance and they all had failed miserably as responsible dog owners.

Ledford brought out the dog's bowls, toys, leash and a giant sack of kibble before bringing me the dog. When I opened up the passenger side of the truck, Bear, now officially renamed Simon, jumped up in the seat as if he had been doing it all his life.

Ledford looked a little sheepish as we pulled away from the house, but the big dog didn't seem to care. "Hasta la vista, Amigo," I said, letting out a loud howl. Simon joined me as if celebrating his freedom. "Welcome to your new life, boy," I said placing a kiss on his big black head.

~

Simon and I quickly settled into a familiar routine over the next three months. Not surprisingly, he never seemed to miss the Langston family. Autumn brought cooler temperatures and we enjoyed our frequent romps on hiking trails and in dog parks. For once in my life, I felt confident that I could finally fulfill my commitment to one of man's best friends. Or so I firmly believed.

It was a Sunday in mid-November and the oppressive southern heat had been replaced by a welcome Canadian cold front. Simon and I took advantage of this, taking a ride one half hour away to a state park Simon loved. I'd looked forward to a good workout; fit, ready for a brisk walk, led by my energetic dog.

About twenty minutes into our walk, I let Simon off-leash. It was then that I become light-headed, a weird tingling sensation slowly spreading throughout my left arm that held the unused leash. "Easy boy," I spoke to Simon who was a few paces ahead. I searched for a place to sit, but it was too late; I fell to the ground landing on my back.

The shadow of the dog's big body crossed my face. His yelps of distress brought fellow-hikers running to help. Simon circled around me, confused, barking at the people who now crowded around. Someone was calling 9-1-1 while someone else administered CPR.

And then Simon disappeared and so did I.

~

The processing area of the afterlife looks like the lobby of one of those giant multi-plex theatres, but in this case it's a venue that shows hundreds of thousands of movies at any given time, 'round the clock. Complete with red carpet, there are countless entrances leading into what looks like an enormous movie screening area, minus the concession stand. This theatre presents the moving images of one's former life that continue to unfold without you.

A young man named Chad, dressed in a black T-shirt and jeans approached me. He carried a clipboard. Without fanfare, he told me that my life on earth had expired and I had a few decisions to make.

He explained how things worked. If I chose to, I could have the opportunity to have a seat in the Life-Viewing Room and watch the people I cared about for as long as I liked. Or I could move along and choose a re-assignment for my next life.

Choosing Option A, I asked Chad, "Does who I choose to watch have to be human?" Chad smiled knowingly and answered, "No sir, you would be surprised how many people choose to watch over their pets."

Chad led me into a cavern of darkness, shining a flashlight like an usher at a Broadway show. In the blackness you almost believed you were alone, unaware of the thousands of others staring up at a tremendous screen.

Chad sat me down and connected a small black box with a panel of buttons to my seat.

"What's that?" I inquired.

"This is what we call an Energy Unit Box." He fiddled with the box and continued to explain. "Based on the quality of the connections you've made with others during the course of your most recent lifetime, you've built up a reserve of emotional energy units that allow you to make visits to the ones you've left behind."

"Is that why people see spirits, or ghosts?"

"That would explain it."

"How many units do I have, exactly?"

Chad looked at me unapologetically. "Not a whole lot. In fact, if it wasn't for Simon you'd have just about none."

He pointed to the control panel of the box. "When you press the Release Button right here, you can transport yourself back down to earth. You arrive wherever you wish to visit. This green button you can use to control the strength of your visibility, or conserve your energy. Remember, you get to choose to whom you wish to appear and how clearly. But choose wisely, like I said, your energy supply is limited."

Yes, Chad had made it painfully clear that I had a deficit of personal connections.

It was a busy day and the efficient young man went off to welcome another newcomer. I took a seat. When I looked up at the screen, I was surprised to see it had come alive with the vision of Simon. As if installed with an inner compass that guided him true north, he wandered along Route I-95, headed for South Carolina.

~

In all the commotion immediately following my demise back in the park, no one had noticed Simon as he slipped away and headed into the woods, scared and confused. His red leash still gripped by my lifeless hand was the only clue that a dog had even accompanied me.

Simon roamed for hours. Now tired and hungry, he sniffed around the in the backyard of the Stephen's residence. Claire Stephen's ten-year old son, Kyle, spotted the big dog just as the starving canine knocked over a large garbage can and rummaged through its spilled contents.

"Bear!" the young boy shouted, running for his mother.

Through the screen door, Claire was relieved to see that Simon was actually a dog that just resembled a bear in the waning light of day. As she cautiously opened the screen door; Simon sauntered into the kitchen, and their hearts.

"He's got a collar on," Kyle said.

Claire noted Simon's name and the phone number.

"What if he's one of those abandoned dogs?" Kyle asked. "You know like by those people who lose their homes." Claire was painfully aware of "those people" her son referred to as she had been slowly losing her own battle to keep her home over the past few months.

Kyle had wanted a dog so badly, he had asked for one often. Claire promised herself she would call the number on the dog's collar the very next morning. But she was in no rush. Things had been so difficult for her boy; she was delighted to see the happiness this dog brought him.

After dinner, Claire and Kyle headed to a pet supply store for a large bag of kibble, a leash, and some squeaky toys at the local dollar store. The next morning Claire thought about making that call, but with each passing day she found a reason to delay in the smile on her son's face.

As the days passed, Claire half-heartedly looked for postings of missing dogs on telephone poles, on Craig's list, and in the newspaper, but saw nothing about a big missing black dog that resembled a bear cub.

~

I have to admit, this downtrodden single mother really had tried to do right by Simon. And watching my dog spend his first night in that house curled up next to Kyle had initially made me happy, too.

At first all appeared to be peaceful in this home. I was glad to see the house had a large, well-maintained fenced backyard for Simon to romp in. But with a little detective work, I'd quickly learned something was amiss.

In the master bedroom where Claire slept alone, a half-empty bottle of vodka and an empty glass sat on the nightstand. This caused me great concern and prompted further investigation. Downstairs, on the kitchen counter, unemployment check stubs and unpaid bills spilled out of a basket. On closer inspection, I saw several marked in bright red as "past due."

But it was a document with a warning about a pending foreclosure that made my heart sink. It appeared that Simon had walked himself right into another precarious situation.

In the weeks that followed, I watched as Claire lost her battle of the bills, and chose to abandon her home instead of being evicted. On a cold mid-December morning Claire and Kyle stood on the front stoops, suitcases in hand. An artificial Christmas wreath hanging on the door gave the scene an odd sense of normalcy.

"But what about Simon?" Kyle said, sniffing back tears.

They were headed for a temporary stay with a friend who had a small rented apartment. "You know we can't have a dog where we're going," Claire answered, sorrow in her voice.

It had angered me that she had done so little about finding a good home for Simon. But I knew that in her current state of despair Claire had managed the best she could. By the time she had gotten around to calling my house phone, it had been disconnected. Beaten down by her circumstances she hadn't been able to find a good home for her son, let alone one for a dog.

Not wanting to surrender him to a shelter, she'd placed a large plastic toy castle lined with blankets in the backyard with as much food and water as possible. Claire believed Simon would be better off outside, where someone might eventually rescue him.

Simon was okay for the first two days, but on the third, his fretful whining and barking grew constant. A mangy tiger-striped cat that lived next door had taken to sitting on the fence further tormenting him. To make matters worse the cat's owner, a cantankerous old coot, screamed at Simon making constant threats.

"Shut up you stupid mutt or I'll come over there and do it myself," he screamed several times each day.

On the fourth day I could stand it no longer. I had to find a way to free Simon from his backyard prison. If ever there was a time for me to use those stupid energy units, it was now.

I pressed the red "Release" button on the side of my chair and found myself just outside the house's fenced yard. Working quickly, I unlocked the gate and let it swing open. I chose to remain invisible, slipping the collar off the confused dog's neck. Just then the neighbor's old cat took its perch on the fence with perfect timing. I walked over and placed my face just inches away from him.

"Boo!" I hissed at the cat, suddenly appearing before him. It worked. The terrified feline, with every hair on its back raised up and its tail flaring, sprinted toward the woods with me in full chase. Simon quickly followed trailing me for about a mile. I disappeared when I felt he had wondered far enough from the house and wouldn't try to return to its awful backyard.

Satisfied that my Energy Units had been put to good use, I returned to my seat in the theatre.

~

Near mid-night, Jill Johnston sat at her computer, a large globe of red wine by her side. These nights, just a few weeks before her wedding day, she'd found herself increasingly restless and unable to sleep. But it was not a restlessness born out of excitement.

Instead of reviewing her guest list, or pricing discount honeymoon travel packages, Jill again found herself perusing the pages of a website filled with images of adoptable dogs. From her computer screen dozens of furry faces of all size and shape peered at her. If she could have a dog, which one would she choose?

But Jill sighed knowing her dream of dog ownership was just that, a dream. Her fiancé, Doug, hated dogs. Too dirty, too much work, what about allergies and those of their future kids? It was a subject he refused to discuss.

Jill, a sales rep for a wine distributor, had stopped complaining to anyone who would listen. Doug was a great catch, and she was in her mid-thirties. Who would sympathize with her about something as trivial as the lack of a family dog?

Jill's eyes came to rest on a close-up image of Simon. The big guy who had been rescued in the backwoods of South Carolina now found himself fostered by someone in New York State. Without any identification he had once again been named Bear by his rescuers, correctly identified as a pure-bred Bouvier de Flandres.

Jill was busy at work taste-testing a bottle of Beaujolais, a light red wine from central France. When she returned to the image of the big black dog, her finger reached out and touched the screen. I knew something was up.

"You're the most beautiful dog I've ever seen," she whispered reaching for her glass. "Boo-vee-yay," she said, laughing, then "Boo-jo-lay." She drained the last of the crimson liquid.

In her wine-inspired state, she'd e-mailed the contact for "Bear's" foster home, inquiring of his status. As she fell asleep that night the last words out of her mouth were, "Simon. Simon de Bouvier," that's what I'll call you. Later, she dreamed of frolicking on a white sandy beach and swimming in an impossibly blue aquamarine ocean with the big black dog instead of her fiancé.

The next morning Jill was excited to see a reply from Simon's foster family among her e-mails. "Yes, Simon is still in need of a good home," it read. The writer went on to explain that he had been found running alongside I-95 in South Carolina and was rescued from a shelter down there just in time. "As you may know, large older dogs, especially those that are black, are the most difficult to place so your inquiry is of great importance to us."

Just in time. Those words haunted Jill. She had then made arrangements to visit the dog the very next day.

Early that morning, a Saturday, Jill cancelled a fitting for her wedding dress and a lunch date with some of her bridal party, feigning illness. Then she hastily packed a suitcase, jumped into her SUV and programmed her GPS for the quickest route to a little town just northeast of Albany, New York.

~

As I watched from my seat in the viewing room, I made a diagnosis. This young woman was dealing with a terrible case of dog fever. I knew from personal experience, she was desperately trying to reclaim a passion in her life before it was siphoned off by a sterile, lifeless routine of life with the dog-despising Doug. I could only wait and hope that she would succeed as my Simon's life now appeared to depend on it.

With her impulsive action, Jill had not stopped to think about the weather in Upstate New York during the month of January. And as luck would have it, she was heading right into a monster of a storm.

Upon her arrival just outside of Cambridge, New York, she pulled off Interstate 287 into the parking lot of a little place called The Winking Moon Motel just as the first flakes began to fall.

"If you're hungry sweetie, ya might want to get yourself over to the diner across the way before you get snowed under," a gray-haired woman in the motel's front office advised Jill as she checked in.

Jill took that advice and within moments was sitting in a red vinyl booth in the back of the Jack Frost Diner. Abandoning her pre-wedding diet, she ordered a bacon cheeseburger with fries, coffee and pie alamode, before placing a call to her sister, Diana.

"Where the hell are you?" were the first words out of sister's mouth.

"I'm eating at a swank restaurant off 287 outside of Albany, New York," Jill answered honestly. "And I have a date with a dog."

"No. Really!" she said. "Doug's coming home early from his business trip and he's been calling all over looking for you. He said he can't reach you on your cell."

Jill had purposely turned off her phone, delaying the inevitable fib she would have to use on her husband-to-be.

"I'm up here to adopt a dog," Jill said. "He's big and beautiful and right now I'm feeling better about life than I have for a long time."

"Jesus," Diana said. "Are you talking about a dog-dog or another man? I really hope it's not a real dog, you know how Doug feels about dogs. He doesn't even want my Bichon in his driveway!"

"You'll love Simon," Jill continued. "You can dog sit when I go on my Honeymoon."

"If you bring that dog back, there won't be any Honeymoon," her sister prophesized. "Look, this might not be the right time to say this, but certainly there must be a way you can have a loving husband, and a loving pooch. If you ask me, the dog is just part of some bigger issues."

Jill sighed. She knew her sister was right, but she didn't want to deal with those issues at the moment. She ended their conversation, pausing just a moment before placing a call to the Bovino residence where Simon was being fostered.

"Hello," the voice of a man answered.

"Yes," she began shakily. "I'm Jill, the person who is here to adopt the Bouvier."

"Well, it's too late," the man said. "He's been adopted."

Jill found it hard to speak. "Wh... What? But I drove all the way up from New Jersey just to see him," she stammered.

On the other end of the line, the man let out a laugh. "Just joking," he said. "I love that dog. I hate to see someone take him from me."

"Give me that phone, Mark," Jill heard the voice of a woman now.

"I'm sorry about that. My brother thinks he's funny. If he had his way he would keep every dog we foster," she explained. "I'm Kelly, Simon's foster mom."

Jill let out a sigh of relief before finding her voice. "I can come over to see him tomorrow. I'm staying at the Winking Moon."

"Looks like you're going to get snowed in. I'll send my brother over to plow you out in the morning. You won't be able to get out of the driveway let alone handle these roads."

When Jill hung up, she finished every last morsel on her plate and ordered a hot chocolate to go before paying her bill.

Up on the viewing screen, I watched this young woman with curious delight as she trudged slowly back to the motel in the deepening snow. Bundled up in her coat and scarf, a smile remained pasted on her face all the way back to her room.

Back at the motel, Jill finally called her fiancé. She claimed to have a bad case of the flu. Knowing Doug's fear of germs, and his lack of care-giving skills, Jill knew this health report would keep him at bay. For good measure, she sneezed directly into the phone several times.

That night, Jill was so excited about the prospect of finally being able to cuddle with her new dog and so oddly curious about what this dog-loving young man looked like, she barely slept. Waking up before sunrise she discovered she was unable to open her motel door now blocked shut by drifting snow. Frustrated, Jill waited to be dug out. I've come to rescue a dog, now I'm the one needing to be rescued.

By eight o'clock that morning, the big dig-out began. From outside Jill heard the sounds of shovels hacking into snow mounds followed by the idling of a big truck and the scraping of a plow's blade on the motel's snow covered parking lot. Her heart raced. She peeked out the motel window just as the snow slid from the motel's sign, and the newly cleared image of the full moon winked down at her again.

She threw on her coat and opened the door, only to be assaulted by icy winds. As if on cue, a tall lanky young man approached and grabbed her bags. "Quick. Follow me," he called back to her, motioning her into the passenger side of his truck. No introduction was necessary.

Jill crawled into the warm vehicle while Mark finished clearing snow from the motel's entrance. His work finished, he jumped into the truck. "I don't usually go through so much trouble to help the person here to take my dog," he said, flashing Jill a warm and perfect smile. When he removed his gloves, Jill found herself examining his left hand for a ring, strangely relieved to find none.

Instead of saying something clever she began to sneeze, this time for real. "I sure hope I'm not coming down with anything."

"Probably just the heat from the vent," he said. "But here, take this. It's a zinc tablet with Vitamin C, just in case."

In the viewing room of the Theater of Life something odd began to happen up on the big screen. The edges of the scenes I was watching began to blur and then to expand. It now appeared that the man two seats down from me was sharing my screen, watching the same series of events unfold. He turned his head toward me as if to acknowledge this.

~

By the time Jill arrived at the Bovino house her heart was beating out of control. And it wasn't just because of the dog.

"There's our boy," Mark said, pointing to a large snow-covered yard. From the seat of the truck, Jill quietly watched as Simon gallivanted happily with a Great Dane and what looked like two mastiffs.

"My sister's a sucker for large breeds," Mark explained. "Unfortunately they're the hardest to place." He pointed at the big bear-like black dog. "A dog like that gets harder to place as he gets bigger and older. He looks to be almost a year old, so his future's in jeopardy."

Jill got out of the car and walked into the yard. Without warning "Simon" charged right for her, just as he had done to me at the Langston home that hot August day. In a matter of seconds, the young woman was flat on her back in the snow with the dog on top of her.

"Bear! Get off," Mark yelled. "Sorry. He needs to work on his greeting skills." But Jill didn't seem to care. She quickly got to her feet and wrapped her arms around the dog's massive chest.

Once inside the Bovino home Jill became flushed with fever and I knew it wasn't just from the excitement of meeting my Simon. Kelly insisted Jill take two aspirin and a nap, announcing that more snow was on the way. "You're stuck here so go rest. You can play with the dog later."

Later that evening Jill made it to the table for dinner. Bear, now officially renamed Simon came and placed his head on her feet underneath the kitchen table. "I see you two are bonding already," Mark said.

Jill ate what she could and excused herself. She headed toward her room with Simon right behind her. It was there that the lonely dog and his new mistress sealed the deal. Simon slept through the night drooling on the pillow right next to Jill's head.

By the next morning, the color had returned to Jill's face. She smiled readily upon discovering Simon had spent the entire night with her. Simon seemed to respond to her renewed energy. He happily followed her every move and he wasn't the only one.

~

It was at this point I took the initiative to speak to the silent man in the viewing room who appeared to be now sharing the screen with me. "Is Mark your boy?" I asked.

"Yes. Mark was, I mean, is my son," he said, correcting himself. "Is Jill your girl?"

I let out a small laugh of embarrassment, having to explain that I was watching my dog in the afterlife and not one of my kids. "No," I replied. "But that dog is my beloved Simon, he knows me better than my son."

"My name's Ed," he said, leaning over to shake my hand. Ed and I reclined in our theatre seats, a silent partnership forming.

"I sure hope your dog ends up with that nice lady," Ed spoke.

"So do I. That poor dog has spent most of his short life looking for a good home," I answered. "This will be his fourth."

This statement recalled the words spoken by my waiter, Oscar, on the porch in Mexico. Yes. This could be Simon's fourth and true home; his casa verdad.

My son Mark always wanted to be a chef and live somewhere warm," Ed continued to speak. "I made him go to college to become an engineer, but he fought it all the way. When I passed a year ago, he used his inheritance to go to culinary school, now he's looking for a position as a chef." Ed paused here, choosing his words carefully. "I know now that you should never try to tell someone what it is they want or don't want to do with their life."

I listened to his words of belatedly acquired wisdom, shifting in my seat. I thought about how Jill was learning that same hard truth for herself through this man's son and my dog.

I don't know if you're a praying man," Ed said to me. "But sometimes, I recite the prayer to St. Anthony when I've lost something. As it appears to me, that you've been trying to find a good home for your "lost" dog, it just might help."

In the darkness Ed, recited for me his version of the prayer. "Tony, Tony turn around, something's lost and must be found."

~

Jill, Mark and Simon spent three full days getting to know each other. Jill was happy to help Mark feed, brush and play with the eight large breed foster dogs. By her laughs and smiles, I knew it was the most fun she had enjoyed in a long time.

I must admit, during this time, I had taken up the practice of reciting that prayer of Ed's to myself. Tony, Tony turn around... I knew in many ways, it was said for the benefit of both dog and some special humans searching for things they had all lost; a good home, abandoned dreams, and the right to live a life that has purpose and meaning. Something's lost and must be found...

During this time Mark told Jill about his dreams of preparing exotic meals, living in some far off place where snow never fell and ice never formed. She, in turn, found herself longing to join him, confiding in the young man her doubts about her upcoming wedding and her simple desire to be married to a man who would accept a dog into their home.

Jill left New York State without a dog, but happy nonetheless. "You can't bring him into another unsettled situation," Mark advised her. "It will only make your situation and the dog's worse."

As much as she wanted to leave with Simon, Jill knew Mark was right. She had a few things to take care of when she got home, and it wasn't going to be pretty. She left empty-leashed under one condition. "Please keep Simon for as long as you can," she had requested of Mark before heading south.

"Don't worry," he assured her. "I won't give our dog away."

Upon her return home Jill embarked on the difficult task of unplanning her wedding and dealing with the aftermath of her decision. Mark had kept his word, regarding Simon now as a permanent fixture rather than a foster. He finished his apprentice work in the kitchen of a local hotel and through the school's job placement service had learned of an inn up for sale just outside of Playa del Carmen called La Casa del Perro Feliz. With a name like that he couldn't resist.

With his inheritance and Jill's encouragement, he'd purchased the place. Jill left her job, packed up and tried to make her peace with those who still didn't quite understand her actions.

"See, you can find a man who wants to share his home with a dog," her sister said. "And he can cook, too!"

After getting Simon's health certificate updated, Jill and Simon made their move together, heading south of the border by early spring.

~

The wedding of Jill Johnston and Mark Bovino took place one year later on the beach of Playa Del Carmen. It was a small affair; a gathering of close friends and immediate family.

Jill, with her long dark hair brushing her tanned shoulders, looked beautiful in a simple white sundress. Mark, bronzed and handsome, wore a tuxedo jacket over shorts and Simon, nearly full grown now, sported a goofy kid-sized sombrero that he good naturedly tolerated.

Ed and I had watched the entire ceremony. "Well, it's time for me to be moving on," Ed proclaimed after the couple exchange vows. "My boy's happy now, and so are Jill and your Simon." He stood and extended his hand. "I'd give you some of my energy units, but I don't think they're transferable."

But I wasn't ready to leave just then. I shook Ed's hand and said I wanted to watch Simon enjoy his new home for a little while, and so I did.

The inn had been open for business for several months now, and the place was booked solid with warmth seeking vacationers. Jill had taken over the administrative functions of the inn and was the resident wine expert, while Mark, and the husband and wife team of Oscar and Concetta, worked non-stop in the kitchen creating award-winning culinary creations.

On this particular morning the tables on the front porch were all occupied. Simon was napping, curled up in a shady corner oblivious to all. Then Oscar came out onto the porch with a plateful of eggs and refried beans, but it wasn't for a customer. Instead, he approached Simon offering the food to the sleepy dog, which he readily inhaled.

Then I realized that I still had a trace of those energy units remaining and I knew just what I wanted to do with them. I pressed the Release button and found myself on the porch of La Casa del Perro Feliz, right between Simon and Oscar.

"Watch it, you know what happens when you give beans to a dog," I whispered loudly, making myself clearly visible.

Simon jumped up startled. Confused, he looked in my direction.

Oscar muttered, "My God," crossing himself.

Simon let out a plaintive whine and a loud sound accompanied by a foul odor.

"Simon, no!" Oscar cried, shooing him off the porch. He turned to me, nodding in disbelief. "Mr. Thomas," he spoke softly. "This perro is muy especial. He has made the house happy again."

"And I am very happy, too," I said' feeling the last of my energy dissipate.

I left the porch, no longer visible and followed Simon. As he bumbled over the warm sand; he nearly trampled a slow-moving iguana in his path. He stopped abruptly near the edge of the impossible blue sea, in the shade of a palm tree, still no lover of water.

As he watched Jill enjoying her morning swim, he was quickly joined by two scraggly mixed breeds similar to the dogs I had tried to feed during my prior visit. All three joined in a chorus of barks, yips and howls as Jill swam for shore. "Okay, Okay," she yelled between strokes.

He has made the house happy again. What Oscar had said to me was true; some dogs really were destined to live under the roofs of three houses before calling the fourth one home.

I thought about a puppy shop somewhere in a flea market in Florida, then about Simon's first "real" home with Ledford Langston in Georgia and those fake palm trees. I wondered if Claire and her son had found a place to live somewhere in South Carolina. I recalled how for a brief time that big dog had found a loving second home with me.

But mostly I enjoyed this special moment watching Simon romping on the beach with his new friends. He had brought so much love into this, his true home; a home that had started in the frosty climes of the Northeast and now brought him to La Casa del Perro Feliz.

Maybe the name of the inn wasn't quite accurate, though. Perhaps it should be renamed El Perro del Casa Feliz, The Dog of the Happy House. For while it was possible for a dog like Simon to find true happiness in a good and forever home, in the end it was the house and the people in it who were the happiest for it.

Still Life with Dog in Red Collar

"What exactly have you been learning in that art room anyway, Kevin?" My father talked at me from across the breakfast table on this warm mid-September morning.

I chose not to answer.

"You have to start focusing on your S. A. T.'s. In case you've forgotten you'll be retaking them soon. Your last scores weren't exactly spectacular."

Exactly was a meaningful word for my father, a Certified Public Accountant. In his world, exactly was a word that fit. And as to his question, I couldn't exactly explain what I was learning in that art room. But I was well aware that I wasn't the conventional college-bound A-plus son he desired.

Despite my silence, he persisted. "By the way, how are we doing in our S. A. T. prep classes?"

We? Our? I wanted to say. But I just managed an "Okay."

Lately, it seemed the inhabitants of my universe were so hung up on S. A. T. scores, grades and choosing the right colleges. It all seemed pointless to me because most of my classmates didn't even have a clue as to what they wanted to do with their lives. At least I did.

I knew the real purpose of this conversation was to further discourage my career choice of becoming a fine artist. A fine lawyer or even a fine investment banker was more to his liking, something he deemed safe and sound. I knew he was only thinking of my welfare, but the subject was getting old.

"My art teacher, Mrs. Turner, said I have a good chance at an art scholarship if I turn in a strong senior project for my portfolio," I said. "Or I can enlist in the military and go to Afghanistan."

My strategy worked. My father stood up so fast he knocked over his chair. He slammed down his coffee mug, breaking off its handle.

"Damn hand-made pottery," he muttered for my benefit. It had been purchased by me last June as a Father's Day gift at a local arts and crafts fair.

He stormed out of the room, but hurried back to the kitchen, groping through a messy stack of papers and junk mail for his car keys. He seemed eager to escape to the sanctuary of his orderly office several safe miles away. "And since you brought it up, how are you doing on that senior art project of yours anyway?" He spoke to me over his shoulder, just before making his final exit.

"Good," I answered, a little too quickly.

Mrs. Turner's encouragement and praise throughout the past three years had fueled my desire to seriously pursue a career in art. But the truth was I had not found much creative inspiration during the long summer break. How could I, in this environment?

Later that day it became apparent that I was dealing with a serious creative block. The conversation begun earlier with my father had now followed me to the school's art room. "Kevin, what's going on with your scholarship project?" Mrs. Turner asked, sneaking up on me as silently as a cat.

I said nothing. How could I tell her I hadn't even chosen a medium or subject yet?

"Focus on your strengths. You're a talented painter," she said as if reading my thoughts. "Just get started and stop hiding your light under a barrel."

But what would I paint? I had grown tired of meaningless still life compositions, bowls brimming with boring green and red apples and pale yellow roses.

I poked half-heartedly at a glob of cerulean blue paint on a clean palette with a stiff new brush, staring at a white canvas. A rap at the window startled me. I looked up to see the face of my good friend, Tommy.

"Hi Kev," he shouted. His blond head was partially concealed by a faded mural painted on the windowpane; a sappy mountain scene I had helped to create during my freshman year.

"Me and John are headed to the marina after school," he spoke quickly. "Meet us there at three. We're going fishing."

From across the room, Mrs. Turner cleared her throat, continuing to advise me. "Guard against outside distractions," she warned. But Tommy had already ducked out of sight and I returned to staring at my blank canvas.

After school, I wandered toward the marina. I knew I should have been heading for home to look at the college brochures my father had collected for me. But it was one of those late summer afternoons, just before the leaves began to turn. I knew these days were numbered.

I entered the park next to the marina and stood at the edge of the river, its murky brown water flowed like a stream of spilled flat cola. Pausing to admire the scene of a brilliant blue sky dotted with huge white clouds rimmed in gray, my eye caught the movement of a black dog darting among a wooded area. He looked like some kind of lab-mix.

"Hey Kev, over here," Tommy yelled, distracting me. He was on board his father's boat handing a fishing rod and bucket to John. Further down the dock, a group of young kids squealed with laughter. They struggled with a heavy crab trap, trying to yank it free from the shallow river bottom. Two tiny blue-clawed crabs had escaped and skittered off the dock. They plopped back into the river to temporary safety.

I started to walk over to the dock, but something else now had my full attention; in the center of a circular rock garden, just a few yards from where I stood, appeared the image of an angel. I recalled that this statue had been erected sometime during the summer, but I had never even taken the time to notice.

The angel was on her knees, hunched over a pedestal engraved with the names of local people who had perished a year earlier on September eleventh. The skilled hand of the sculptor had convincingly conveyed the angel's pain through her slumped posture and folded wings. She had been caught off guard. Her head hung in sorrow over the etched image of the World Trade Center.

"Yo man, what are you doing? C'mon!" Tommy's voice carried over to me from the dock. But inspiration had struck. I recalled Mrs. Turner's warning about outside distractions. There was no time to explain to my friend; somehow I knew he wouldn't understand.

"Got to go," I answered, waving and running away from the dock and out of the park.

At home I gathered up my sketchpad, a handful of charcoal pencils and a tin of watercolors. I almost escaped out the back door unnoticed.

"Kevin, what about those applications?" my mom called from upstairs. "You promised your father."

"I'll look at them tonight. Gotta go, can't lose the light."

Back at the park, the dock was quiet now; Tommy and John had gone fishing. I sketched quickly, using the watercolors to make color notes.

It was then that I again noticed the big black dog. This time, he came out of the woods and stood just yards away from where I worked, watching my every move. He wore no collar.

"Here, boy," I spoke to him. But the skittish dog kept its distance, circling me a few times before disappearing into a stand of pine and pin oak. I wondered if he had a home.

The following day in the art room, I worked with a new energy. Prepping a canvas, I began my preliminary drawing. Mrs. Turner smiled and nodded in my direction. But my newfound enthusiasm faded as I rehashed the previous morning's confrontation at home.

Scribble, sketch, scribble, and sigh. My inspiration drained as the classroom clock methodically ticked away the minutes. Safe-sound, safe-sound, it taunted, delivering a message from my father.

My change in mood hadn't gone unnoticed by my teacher. "Kevin, you have a tendency to discourage too easily. You see your work finished before you've even taken the time to lay the foundation."

I put my brush down. I would try again later.

"Keep your eye on the big picture and worry about the details later," she offered. "Don't worry so much about the final result. Things have a way of working out."

I knew she was right, but the next few days weren't much different. I was beginning to think like my father, stuck in a negative place.

To get out of my funk, I returned to work at the place that had inspired me; at the riverfront in the park. It was the first day of autumn and with the cooler weather, the park was nearly empty. But the slight chill in the air served as a reminder of my approaching deadline.

Before I set up to work, I walked up to the statue, really looking at it for the first time as more than just my subject matter. Carefully reading each name etched on her pedestal, I traced the raised letters with my fingertips.

One man's name stood out. A financial advisor, he had been the uncle of one of my classmates. A talented photographer, I recalled reading in his obituary he had hoped one day to pursue his real passion to become a full-time photographer. I was struck by the realization that his "one-day" would never come.

I walked down to the sandy edge of the river. A thicket of sumac cast a crimson blush on the water, its surface smooth like a mirror. From across the river, a woman called her family to dinner, a dog barked and lights slowly came on in windows like tiny candles. At that moment, my mind was as still as the water below me, and the statue that loomed behind me.

I was holding my breath. When I stooped down to examine the image of my face, I exhaled slowly causing a slight ripple to run across my reflection. With my finger, I traced the outline of my likeness in the cool water, as I had done with the names on the statue. I realized now that despite my father's well-meaning concerns, in today's world, there was no such thing as a safe choice. I knew then that this would be the start of my "one-day."

Returning to my easel, I discovered someone had placed baskets of orange and white chrysanthemums near the base of the angel's pedestal. Amid the faded summer-weary impatiens and geraniums, their freshness stood out.

I started to paint with a purpose. I don't know how long I worked, but when I looked up from my easel I noticed that the black dog was now sitting among the flowers at the base of the pedestal. He looked directly at me as if posing.

"What is it boy?" I asked. "Do you want to be part of the picture, too?" He sat as still as the statue beside him as I sketched his likeness." When I was finished I looked up, but he was gone again, like a phantom.

This dog seemed to be searching for someone who would never arrive. I thought about all the dogs that had waited at home that day after the tragedy in downtown Manhattan, never knowing why their humans had never returned for them.

I recalled reading about the brave search and rescue dogs that had helped in their own special way at the site of the collapsed towers and during the days and weeks afterward. Over three hundred of them; used in the largest canine search and rescue mission in the nation's history, Dobermans, shepherds, retrievers; reaching places where humans could not, tireless, brave, fearless. And when their work was done, offering comfort to their human partners and giving hope to those waiting for some news at home.

I collected my materials and put the canvas away. Looking around, I saw no trace of the dog. I headed home with a renewed conviction about the choices I would now make.

Later that evening, after dinner, I went through the motion of thumbing through slick college catalogues filled with smiling students walking through perfectly landscaped campuses. I even filled out several applications for good measure.

Then, in the privacy of my room, I quietly filled out the form for the art school scholarship I now wanted more than ever. I pictured myself rambling through the gritty streets of a city like New York, portfolio in hand. That image would buoy me during the battles that were sure to come as I stood my ground.

The next day, I approached my work with a newfound energy that would continue throughout the day. Mrs. Turner must have sensed it because she kept her distance while keeping a watchful eye on me.

At the end of the room, Mr. Ed, the custodian, began clearing the old murals from the room's window. The vinegar scent of window cleaner traveled toward me. "Make room for the new," I heard him mutter to no one in particular. With each swipe of his squeegee, he erased a little of my past, where soon some bright new talent would leave his or her mark.

I was so focused on my painting I hardly noticed the acorn that shot through an open window. It bounced off my canvas landing at my feet; a tiny smudge of yellow paint covered its tip. I knew who had thrown it without looking up.

"Hey Picasso!" a voice called. It was Tommy. "How's your masterpiece coming? Let's have a look," he said pushing half his body through the window.

But I wasn't ready to share my work. I took a break and went over to him. He told me about all the fish he and John had caught the day before and their plans to go surfing after school. "Come with us. We're heading out now."

"No thanks, I've got something to finish," I answered.

"Well go kick some scholarship butt, Van Gogh," Tommy said, quickly moving on.

That was good, because I had finally come to the part I still loved best, working on the details. With a tiny brush loaded with burnt sienna, I put the final touch on a pot of chrysanthemums near the angel's knee. But my eye went to the figure of the dog; something was missing. I painted a red collar around its neck. He had now become an official part of the picture, finding a forever home and a place of honor for his fellow canines there on my canvas.

When my painting was finished, I signed it in the lower right hand corner. Then I sat still, silently thanking the sculptor whose own inspired creation had given me a new outlook on life. I offered a moment of silence for those memorialized by this angel, and the thousands of lives lost, or changed forever on that day.

From the back of the room, Mrs. Turner quietly hummed a tune as she shuffled around the room preparing for her next class.

That night I completed my official entry form for the scholarship judging process. On the line requesting the painting's "Title" I neatly printed, Still Life with Dog in Red Collar.

If my father asked me again what I had been learning in that art room, I still didn't know if I could put it into words. But it didn't matter; in my heart I knew. Exactly.

Made in the USA
Charleston, SC
21 July 2012